B

I Bought On eBay

101 Crazy Bizarre, Seriously Weird, Ridiculously Raunchy Items Exposed

CARY MCNEAL AND BEVERLY JENKINS

RUNNING PRESS
PHILADELPHIA • LONDON

© 2011 by Cary McNeal and Beverly Jenkins
A Hollan Publishing, Inc. Concept
Photography © 2011 by Allan Penn, except where otherwise noted

Published by Running Press,
A Member of the Perseus Books Group

All rights reserved under the Pan-American and International
Copyright Conventions
Printed in China

This book may not be reproduced in whole or in part, in any form or by any means, electronic or mechanical, including photocopying, recording, or by any information storage and retrieval system now known or hereafter invented, without written permission from the publisher.

Books published by Running Press are available at special discounts for bulk purchases in the United States by corporations, institutions, and other organizations. For more information, please contact the Special Markets Department at the Perseus Books Group, 2300 Chestnut Street, Suite 200, Philadelphia, PA 19103, or call (800) 810-4145, ext. 5000, or e-mail special.markets@perseusbooks.com.

ISBN 978-0-7624-4184-6
Library of Congress Control Number: 2010940973

9 8 7 6 5 4 3 2 1
Digit on the right indicates the number of this printing

Cover and interior design by Jason Kayser
Edited by Jordana Tusman
Typography: Din

Running Press Book Publishers
2300 Chestnut Street
Philadelphia, PA 19103-4371

Visit us on the web!
www.runningpress.com

Photo Credits:

p. 230: © John Pichler; p. 233, 237, 240, 245: © iStockphoto.com
p. 235: © Steve Pianowski; p. 242: © Shutterstock.com/Alexey Fursov
p. 247: © eBanners @ eBay; p. 248: © Shutterstock.com/Eric Isselée
p. 249, 251: © Jim Rich, CRNA; p. 252: © Don Fox
p. 254: © Ian Roth/eXtremeRestraints.com

CONTENTS

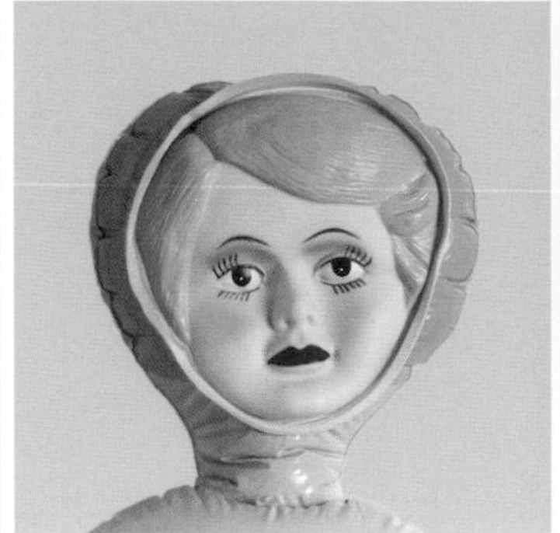

INTRODUCTION

Every day, millions of people from all over the world turn to eBay for their crap-buying and selling needs, often with unintentionally hilarious results. Need a crocheted penis warmer? eBay has 'em. Haunted doll? Take your pick. Jewelry made from animal droppings? Of course.

Just about any hard-to-find, unnecessary, and inexplicable item on your wish list can be found on eBay, the most popular online auction website in history. No, we didn't get paid to write that. But if anyone from eBay is reading this, we certainly wouldn't turn down a small gratuity.

While writing this book, we purchased nearly two hundred items of varying quality and dubious taste from all over the world, and then chose our favorite 101 crappiest pieces. We bought the items because 1) whether it's a dog turd or an eBay purchase, you really need to hold crap in your hand and allow it to violate all of your senses in order to experience the full scope of its craptitude, and 2) *Crap I Saw on eBay but Was Too Cheap to Buy* just doesn't have the same ring to it.

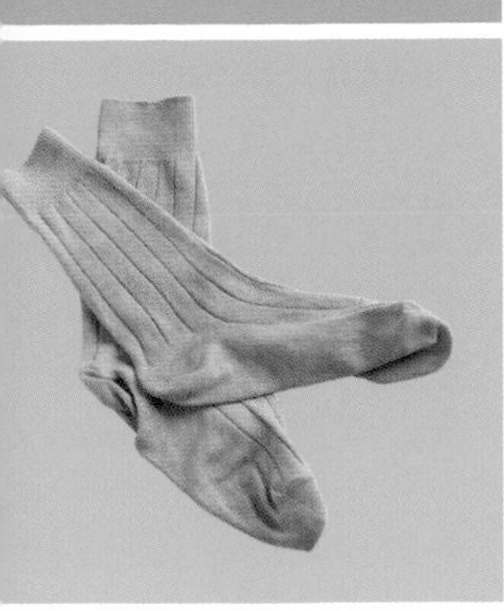

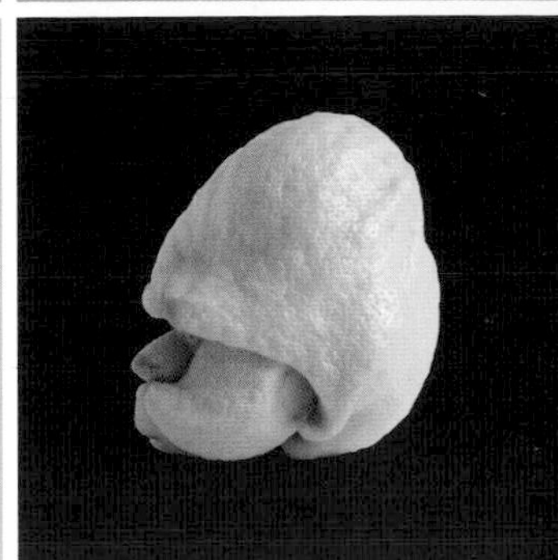

While throwing away our hard-earned money on this crap, we also got an education. We learned that with a simple voodoo spell you can clone yourself. We learned that an animal scrotum can be made into sturdy and attractive leather goods. We learned that war machines, moon property, and entire buildings are all available for the right price. And we learned that people want the freedom to masturbate, fornicate, urinate, and take a dump whenever, wherever, and however they choose, and if they can't find ways to make that happen, they will come up with their own.

We are grateful to all of the sellers who made this book possible by answering our crazy questions and entertaining our bizarre email exchanges. Yes, we were buttholes, but we did call ourselves "S. Finkter," so it's not like you weren't warned. Besides, you have to admit—it sure was fun. Well, for us, anyway.

Craptastically yours,
S. Finkter
(Cary & Bev)

PREVIOUSLY LIVING CRAP

FINAL INDIGNITIES FOR DEAD CRITTERS

Since the dawn of time, mankind has been hunting defenseless animals, wearing their hides as clothing, and displaying their lifeless heads as trophies. But in this day and age, there's still something disturbing about seeing a candy dish made from a bull's nuts or half of a dead squirrel Super Glued to a plaque for display in your man cave. Disturbing, yet hilarious. We're not questioning the art of taxidermy as much as we're wondering who thinks using dead animal parts as tchotchkes is funny. Besides us, that is.

KANGAROO SCROTUM POUCH

LOCATION: Queensland, Australia

COST: $8.99

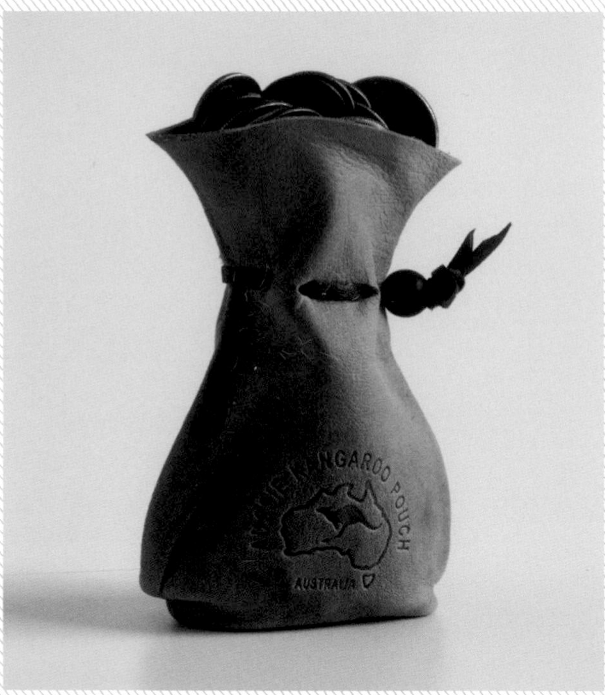

DESCRIPTION:

Real kangaroo scrotum coin purse, tanned in Australia. Roo scrotes have been used for thousands of years by indigenous Australians because of their strength and durability. The perfect coin purse! Once you go scrote, you'll never go broke! The leather is thick and strong (imagine how hard it has to be to support the gonads of a hopping kangaroo!). The size of each purse varies.

We've heard that in Japan, the hand can be used like a knife. And in Australia, a kangaroo's nutsack can be used like a purse. We're not sure how the kangaroo feels about that, but it must not matter because eBay is lousy with these things.

Poor kangaroos. Americans find them cute and quaint, so we imagine them living free and happy down under, spending their days hippity-hopping around the outback, tossing boomerangs, and saying stuff like "A dingo ate my baby!" and laughing it up. Clearly we are mistaken, since we can't think of any definition of a charmed life that includes having your balls cut off and made into leather goods. We wrote the seller to find out how they could get away with this.

↗ Dear Ball Snatcher,

I hope the kangaroo was already dead when you cut off his balls. They will kick the shit out of you.

S. Finkter

↗ Dear S. Finkter,

The animals are quite dead before their testicles are removed, as that would be cruel. We do not kill them. They are culled by the government due to overpopulation.

Ball Snatcher

That would be cruel, says he. As opposed to hacking off their genitals and selling them on eBay as coin purses.

↗ Dear Ball Snatcher,

Gotcha. So how do you pick which scrotums to use? Are there like a bunch of dead kangaroos in a line and you walk along and say, "I'll take his nuts. And his. Not that one, he's too small"?

S. Finkter

↗ Dear S. Finkter,

Ha ha! No, not quite like that. I'll be happy to explain if you are interested in purchasing one.

Ball Snatcher

↗ Dear Ball Snatcher,

That's okay. I will buy one, but I'd rather not know all the lurid details. By the way, there is a dog living next door that I hate. If I sent you his nuts, could you make me a pouch?

S. Finkter

↗ Dear S. Finkter,

Sorry, mate. Only kangaroos. Won't the dog kick the shit out of you? ;)

Ball Snatcher

Good one, mate. Here's an idea: let us do the comedy and you just answer the questions, okay?

2

COWBOY GRAY SQUIRREL HEAD MOUNT

LOCATION: Potosi, MO

COST: $65

DESCRIPTION:

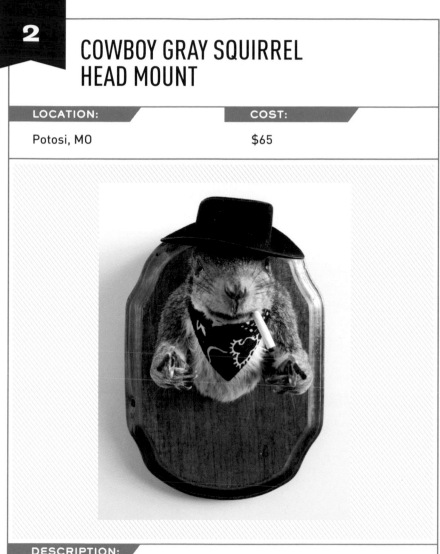

You are bidding on a mounted gray squirrel with a cowboy hat, bandana, 2 toy six shooters, and a cigarette in his mouth (which can be removed). He is mounted on a stained and sealed 5" × 7" wood plaque with a metal hanger on the back.

Howdy, pardners! The name's Roscoe X. Scuriolus, but most people call me Johnny Whiskers. I'm the fastest gun in the East—or used to be, till I got my ass-end blowed off. That's why only half of me is stuck to this plaque. The other half ain't sticking out the back, if you're wondering.

I got shot because I was eating from some guy's bird feeder. Is that so wrong? A squirrel's got to eat. People say, "Can't you find any acorns?"—like that's easy. You ever tried to eat an acorn? It's harder than it looks. The shell is a bitch to crack, and when you finally do, there's one tiny little nut in there. It's like eating crab legs, except when people eat crab legs, they don't have to worry about being caught by a fucking cat.

I had just gotten on the feeder when I heard a loud BLAM!, and then something hit my backside like a sledgehammer. I jumped off the feeder and tried to scurry up a tree but kept slipping, so I look down and I'm like, "Well, hell, no wonder! You got no legs, Rock. You got no back end at all!" Then I died. Squirrel, interrupted.

In hindsight, I'm pretty sure one of my gang sold me out. There's a mole in my bunch, a rat. A couple of chipmunks, too, and a prairie dog, but I've known them for years. I think the rat was the mole. Or the mole was the rat. Note to self: never trust anything that has feet growing out of its head.

So that's my story, kids. Now be smart and learn something from what's left of ol' Johnny Whiskers: crime don't pay. Unless you call being blown in half, stuffed, and mounted on some hillbilly's wall a happy ending.

3

REAL FROG SKIN HALF BODY KEYCHAIN

LOCATION: Port Saint Lucie, FL

COST: $5

DESCRIPTION:

This Key Chain is made of real half body frog skin. Farm raised in the Philippines. A very unique gift! Please send me an email if you have questions or need additional pictures. We also combine shipment.

Quick, name something you have that you most likely touch with your hands every single day. Ew, not that, you pervs! Your keys. Duh. Now imagine holding half of a dead frog in your hand several times a day, cupping that leathery little corpse every time you start your car or let yourself into the house. **shiver**

It's hard to guess what kind of person thinks that having half of a dead frog hanging from their ignition switch is cool, yet somebody must because these little beauties are selling like hotcakes. In fact, there is such a high demand for them that they have entire frog farms in the Philippines where, for pennies a day, workers breed the little buggers, kill them, cut them in half, and stuff the torso and head with sand or sawdust or whatever they use. And you thought *your* job sucked.

You may think that the grossest thing about this truly repulsive item is the glassy fake eyeballs or the weirdly amputated midsection, but you'd be wrong. The most unsettling part is the spindly forearms that seem poised to break off as soon as you touch them.

Of course, we wondered why these frogs have no hindquarters. We pictured a farm full of deformed half frogs specifically bred to become grotesque keychains some day; maybe they scoot around in tiny wheelchairs like those embarrassed-looking handicapped dogs you see every now and then. Time to have a chat with our eBay seller.

↗ Dear Toadilly Creepy,

No legs? Where is the other half of this frog?

S. Finkter

↗ Dear S. Finkter,

I not sure where they go. I buy these already made. Thanks!

Toadilly Creepy

↗ Dear Toadilly Creepy,

Maybe they are eaten? They taste like chicken and are delicious. Could I possibly get the name of your distributor so I can get some legs sent my way? Thanks.

S. Finkter

No answer, so we can only assume that the bottom halves get sent to fancy French restaurants to be consumed by the sort of posh snobs who would never dream of using a dead frog as a keychain. Because that's just gauche.

4

BULL SCROTUM CANDY DISH

LOCATION:

Pennsylvania, USA

COST:

$11.50

BULLIE BAGS
THE BULL STOPS HERE
THE LAST OF THE OLD BULL; THE CAUSE OF IT ALL!

DESCRIPTION:

The item up for auction is a Bullie Bag. It is in very good condition. It is sold out on other web sites. It is a real bull scrotum coated with polyurethane. It can be used as a candy dish.

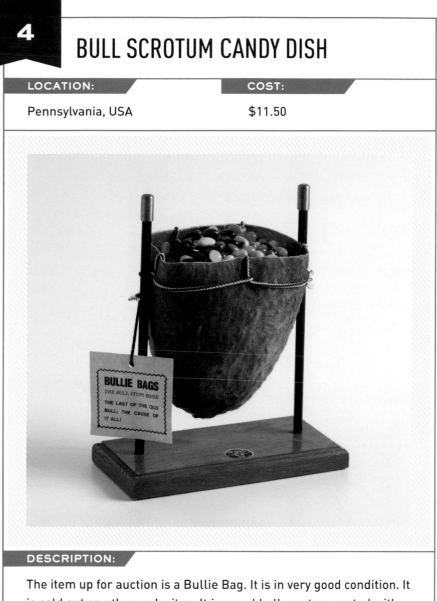

When you're craving that mid-afternoon sugar fix, why not help yourself to some goodies from a hollowed-out bull skin that once contained his testicles? Better yet, offer guests some chocolate truffles and wait until they take a bite to tell them that this candy dish is made out of a ballsack.

You could go the obvious route and store mixed nuts in your Bullie Bag. Or perhaps beef jerky? Peanut M&Ms? Almond Joy (sometimes you feel like a nut!)? The possibilities are limitless!

A quick Internet search will show you that it takes a certified "ballologist" or "shaftologist" to recycle these surplus bull 'nads because, just like snowflakes, no two are exactly alike. They vary in size, shape, and color. Anyone who has ever accidentally walked into a men's locker room or attended one of Elton John's pool parties can tell you that's true of most scrotums, right?

The ad also insists that this is the perfect gift for someone who has everything, but we aren't so sure. We've received some really crappy gifts before—everything from a lint roller to a sweatshirt with puffy frolicking kittens on the front—but never anything that once contained gonads. We tried to imagine the scene as Grandpa unwraps his Bullie Bag in front of the Christmas tree.

GRAMPS

(loudly, because he is hard of hearing)

"Well, good. I needed a new hat."

YOU

"It's not a hat, Grandpa, it's a Bullie Bag!"

GRAMPS

"A wooly what?"

YOU

"A Bullie Bag. It's a candy dish made out of a dried shellacked dead bull's ballsack!"

GRAMPS

"Never read him. I hate the French."

YOU

"Not Balzac! Ball sa—ah, forget it."

A half hour later, you see Gramps wearing the Bullie Bag on his head like a hat. And you just let it go. He's an old man, let him have his fun.

5

REAL HAIR CAT—HANDMADE ANIMAL/PET

LOCATION:

North Carolina, USA

COST:

$19.99

DESCRIPTION:

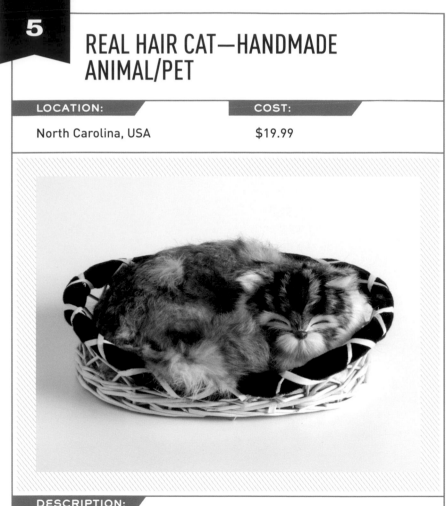

This is the perfect pet!!! No cleaning up after it, no walking it, no bills from the vet, it does not even want food or water. Just about anybody should be able to handle this. This cute cat is handmade and even its hair is real rabbit hair!!! It's almost like the real thing. 10" W × 8" L, MADE BY RABBIT HAIR. No animals were harmed to make these.

Read the description one more time and really let it simmer in the old noggin for a moment. This is a fake cat made out of sawdust and rabbit fur that is designed to trick anyone visiting your home into reaching out and stroking it. Aw! Isn't that cute? Uh, no.

Let's face it: Norman Bates probably made the same cleanliness/easy-to-care-for argument about keeping his petrified dead mother around; why would having a fake cat made out of rabbit fur strike us as any less creepy or gross than seeing Mother propped up in her old-timey rocking chair?

The seller even suggests giving this horrific creation to a child who has been asking for a pet. "Hey Sally, here's a fake stuffed cat covered in the hide of a dead rabbit. I'd get you a real pet, but you might fuck it up, so this is better." Nice.

While we're on the subject of animal cruelty, we thought it was funny that the listing specifically mentioned that no animals were harmed in the making of this mess. Uh huh. *Sure*. The rabbits just *donated* their fur, right?

↗ Dear Cree P. Kitty,

How did the rabbits give you their fur without getting hurt? I thought that only worked for Bugs Bunny.

S. Finkter

↗ Dear S. Finkter,

The rabbits were used for other things and the fur was left over. They don't kill them just for their fur to make these.

Cree P. Kitty

↗ Dear Cree P. Kitty,

So the rabbits are dead?! This is a cat made of dead rabbit fur? WTF?

S. Finkter

↗ Dear S. Finkter,

Yes, but I don't make them myself. I resell them.

Cree P. Kitty

Oh, so that makes killing rabbits for this grotesque Hare Club for Cats okay?

↗ Dear Cree P. Kitty,

I'm sure that makes all the difference in the world to a dead bald rabbit.

S. Finkter

HOME CRAP HOME

FURNISHINGS AND DÉCOR. FROM HELL.

A man's home is his castle, they say, and the place where he can let his freak flag fly with questionable choices in décor and art. For those of you who have chosen *nouveau maison du trailer* as your domestic motif, eBay is your personal nirvana. It's like having every flea market, yard sale, and curbside eviction pile right at your fingertips, and you don't even have to leave the comfort of your prefabricated aluminum house or miss a minute of "Billy the Exterminator." Home *crap* home; because there's nothing *sweet* about this crap.

6

ANGRY VAGINA PAINTING

LOCATION: Brooklyn, NY

COST: $35

DESCRIPTION:

Angry Vagina is an abstract piece of the beauty and rage of woman. With gorgeous colors this piece is an amazing interpretation of woman. Painted on canvas with oil paints. One of a kind piece.

Here's a painting that would make Georgia O'Keeffe jealous. But instead of disguising the subject as a flower, this artist has the courage to call it exactly what it is: a big ol' flaming cooter.

Oh yes, this vagina is seriously pissed off—do the broad, urgent red strokes give it away? The disturbing yellow-orange stripes that hint of infection? Or the random raging pubes uncoiling like a viper to strike anyone in their path?

An angry vagina benefits no one. No one wants to see it. No one wants to talk about it. No one wants to play with it. Women are vengeful, men are denied, and children are beaten and sent to bed without dinner. Everyone suffers. It's like the old saying: when the vagina ain't happy, ain't nobody happy.

We felt it our duty to find out why this minge was miffed, so we contacted the seller.

↗ Dear Bellicose Beaver,

Why is the vagina so angry? Aunt Flo came to town unannounced? Or did someone give it an STD? The yellowish discoloration doesn't look good. You might want to see a gyno.

S. Finkter

↗ Dear S. Finkter,

Vagina was angry because it was having an angry argument with her jerk fiancé, so my mind envisioned an angry vagina. Whenever I am angry I paint with reds and really try to make the canvas explode with color. "Angry Vagina" can also be representative of all the frustrations of being a woman and trying to balance everything on a daily basis.

I do not have an STD.

Bellicose Beaver

Relief. Who wants a painting of diseased genitalia? We're digging that whole "angry vagina as the struggles of womanhood" metaphor, too, so we contacted the artist again.

↗ **Dear Bellicose Beaver,**

Makes total sense. Balancing everything is a challenge, even for a man. I think my penis is angry, too. Do you have any angry penis paintings? If not, mine would be happy to model for you. In fact, he's kind of modeling right now. Would you like to see his head shot?

S. Finkter

No reply. Talk about ungrateful. But that's an angry vagina for you: no manners.

7

TRUCKER JESUS & BIG RIG—VELVET PAINTING

LOCATION:	COST:
Fullerton, CA	$65

DESCRIPTION:

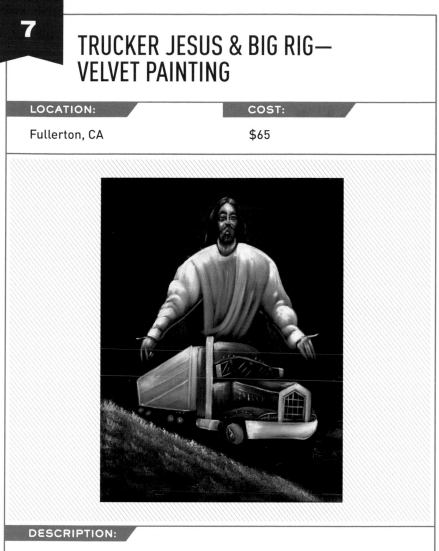

TRUCKER JESUS: HE'S IN IT FOR THE LONG HAUL. This is an original hand-painted authentic Mexican Black Velvet portrait from Tijuana, Mexico of Jesus Christ and an 18-Wheeler Big-Rig. Guaranteed to be entirely hand-painted by professional Mexican velvet artists from Tijuana, Mexico exclusively for you.

Here's a painting that brings to mind one word: *what*. Followed by two more words: *the* and *fuck?!*

We've seen some crazy stuff on velvet before: Elvis welcoming Kurt Cobain to Heaven. Malcolm X and Marilyn Monroe at the Last Supper. Zombie dogs playing poker. And now Trucker Jesus. That's right: Trucker Jesus.

Zombie dogs playing poker, we get, but Jesus and truckers? What's the connection? Even Jesus doesn't know—look at Him. He's holding out his arms as if to say, "I died for *this?* Really??" And if he wasn't Jesus, he'd probably add a "Fuckin' A!"

Don't truckers already have God as their co-pilot? Now they want Jesus, too? Sorry, guys, only one deity per occupation. Besides, you don't need Jesus, *we* do, as in the rest of us who have to share the road with you pill-popping, sleep-deprived menaces. Do you ever wonder what Jesus must think when you fly up on our asses doing ninety, honking and flashing your lights? Or, when you drive up next to us and do that tongue-and-fingers gesture that means you want to go down on us? Or, when you fall asleep at the wheel, veer into our lane, and almost run us into a bridge abutment so we explode and die?

We'll tell you what He thinks: He thinks you're an asshole, just like we do. Because you are. On another note: don'tcha know that Jesus gets sick and tired of being the subject of the world's crappiest art? We would. Especially if the "artist," like this one, gave us googly eyes and mangled hands and made us look more like Duane Allman than the Son of God.

We'd flat smite the shit out of somebody for that.

Someone will be smote for this.

8

FRAMED ORIGINAL ARTWORK: RECLINING CAT

LOCATION:	COST:
White River Junction, VT	$5

DESCRIPTION:

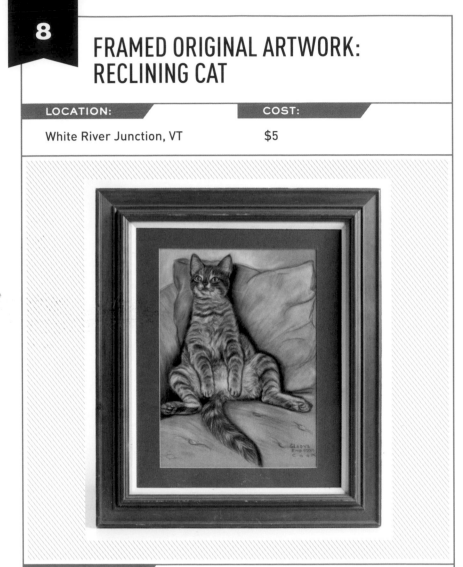

This is a large original work of art by Gladys Cook. It shows a very life-like cat just hanging out with his paws on his tummy. It is pastel on canvas and comes mounted and framed. It is signed by the artist.

You've heard of LOLcat—this is WTFcat.

Take a gander at this fine example of cat breed. The way this pussy is sitting with his legs spread and his little paws on his crotchal region makes him look like a total schlubb—the Al Bundy of the feline world. All that's missing is a remote control and a can of Schlitz. Maybe a stained wifebeater, too. Look at that satisfied look on his face. We've seen that look before—he must have just finished.

Sure, cats sit like this sometimes, we guess. But nobody wants to look at artwork of humans with their gut hanging out and their hands wedged into the waistband of their pants, and the same goes for pets. It would be like capturing the lovely image of our dog licking his balls or our horse unloading a steaming pile of road apples into the dust. We know that these things happen, but we don't need to see them immortalized on canvas. We wrote to the seller to see what she knew about this aesthetic atrocity.

↗ Dear Work O'Fart,

Nice painting. Was it made at the nervous hospital?

S. Finkter

↗ Dear S. Finkter,

Not sure where it was made. I got it at an auction.

Work O'Fart

↗ Dear Work O'Fart,

Mind if I ask why you're selling it? It's so magnificent.

S. Finkter

↗ Dear S. Finkter,

Thank you. I'm selling it because I bought it for my daughter, but she didn't care for it. I'm glad you like it.

Work O'Fart

↗ Dear Work O'Fart,

I never said I liked it.

S. Finkter

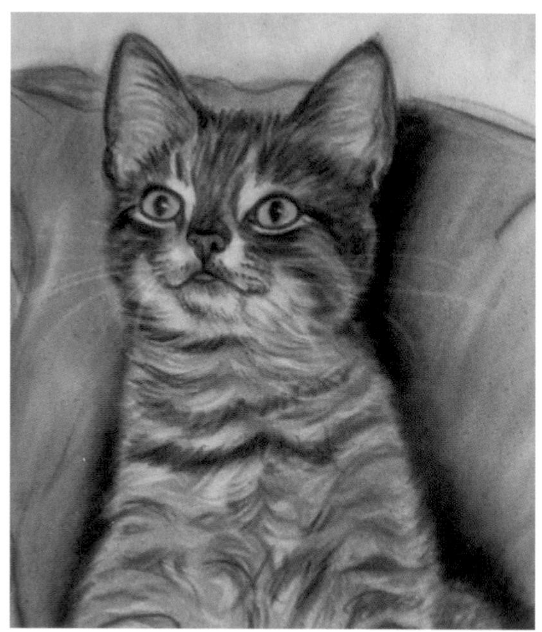

9

VIAGRA CLOCK

LOCATION:

Delmar, NY

COST:

$14.95

DESCRIPTION:

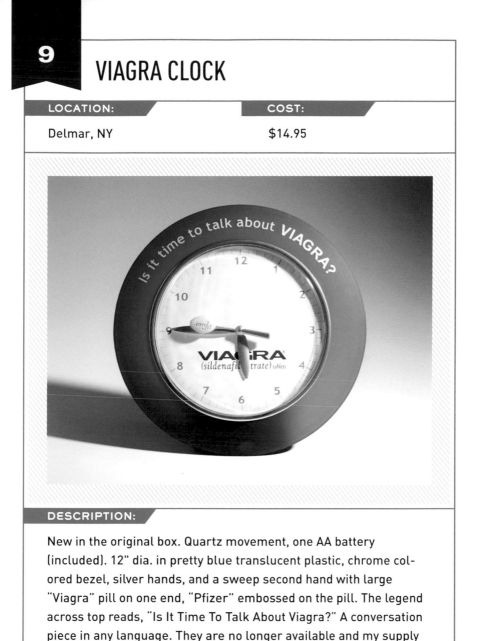

New in the original box. Quartz movement, one AA battery (included). 12" dia. in pretty blue translucent plastic, chrome colored bezel, silver hands, and a sweep second hand with large "Viagra" pill on one end, "Pfizer" embossed on the pill. The legend across top reads, "Is It Time To Talk About Viagra?" A conversation piece in any language. They are no longer available and my supply is limited, so once they are gone, they are gone.

It's eleven o'clock. Do you know where your boner is?

What a thoughtful gift for any man who can't get it up: a glaring reminder that he can't get it up every time he checks to see what time it is. No matter when he looks, it's always half past limp o'clock (o'cock?).

Poor guy—getting old sucks. First your eyes go. Then your ears go. Then your joints go. Then the one thing you thought would never go goes—your ability to get an erection just by looking at the lingerie ads in the Macy's circular or watching the women golfers on TV bend over to pick up their balls.

Fortunately, we now have drugs that can make your dingus hard on command. Unfortunately, even guys who *know* they need boner drugs don't want to admit that they need boner drugs (excluding those idiots in the Viva Viagra commercial who sit around singing about their hard-ons like some demented musical circle-jerk). This is why we end up with things like a clock that wants to shame you into getting help for your erectile dysfunction.

"Is it time to talk about Viagra?" No, clock, it's time to mind your own goddamn business. The seller describes this clock as a conversation piece, and we'll agree with that. Here's that conversation:

Doctor's Office Manager:
"Please tell me you aren't going to hang that thing in here."

Doctor:
"Fuck, no!"

10

WORLD'S MOST HIDEOUS ASHTRAY. SERIOUSLY CRAPPY.

LOCATION: Tempe, AZ

COST: $7.95

DESCRIPTION:

We have decided that this is the world's ugliest ashtray. From its inbred design to its brain-damaged-redneck-on-crack paint job, this is truly one big pile of crap.

We don't know if this is the world's ugliest ashtray or not. We don't even know if it's an ashtray at all. We don't know what the hell it is. It could be an ashtray. It could be a candy dish. It could be an art class project—a Special Ed art class project, that is. For the blind. And mentally challenged. Who have no hands.

Maybe it's a cremation urn. Here lies the Marlboro Man: one bowl for his ashes, one for the ashes of all of the cigarettes he smoked (in fifteen minutes), and one for his mustache, which refused to burn even at a toasty 1,800 degrees in the cremation oven. That's how macho it was. We asked some of our friends what they thought it was, and here's what they said:

"A ceramic ode to *Brokeback Mountain*." —Leisa M.

"Whatever it is, I would sanitize it. Twice." —Erika E.

"Something from the Cracker Barrel gift shop?" —Miguel C.

"A petrified dolphin uterus." —Jeff J.

"Georgia O'Keeffe's only work of mixed media art using Play-Doh, which she called Southwest Vagina Cactus." —Jessica O.

"3 hearts, 1 hat." —Audra M.

"I don't want to know. I'm serious." —Laurie T.

"You paid money for that? Give me a heads-up next time and I'll take a dump and spray paint it for you." —Don C.

"Three heart-shaped hot tubs for those miniature troll dolls. The cowboy hat in the middle is a place for them to set their drinks and snacks and whatnot." —Connie B.

"Did you get this at Helen Keller's yard sale?" —Mr. C.

Whatever it is, it creeps us out. We put it by the street hoping that someone would drive by and take it—everything else we put out there disappears in minutes, even pee-stained mattresses—but this thing sat there for a week. Until early one morning when the CDC van showed up and some guys in Hazmat suits and a forklift scooped it up and took it away.

11

WOOD-CARVED MATING ELEPHANTS

LOCATION:

Duluth, MN

COST:

$12

DESCRIPTION:

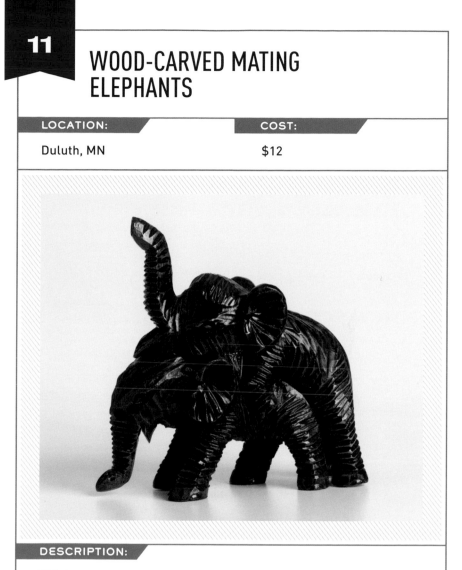

This is a very unique piece. It is a heavy wooden carving of elephants mating. It measures 11" long by 11¼" tall. This is a nice dark wood and very well done.

Sure, elephants are cool, but fucking elephants are even cooler, right? Fuck yeah, that's right.

Here's a sculpture that we bet you didn't even know you wanted until now—the Wood-Carved Mating Elephants statue. This foot-tall hunk of hardwood will add that interesting focal point that your study or office has been lacking, because who among us wouldn't want to look at Babar banging his lady friend like only a thirty-thousand-pound mammal can?

We wondered who would set out to carve such a saucy but inexplicable sculpture. We imagined a tiny raisinlike man in the African bush talking in clicks and grunts as he sharpens his knife and prepares to make some art. Maybe he was searching for inspiration when, lo and behold, he saw it: two elephants making sweet, sweet love under the baking desert sun. He really tried to capture the pained look on the female elephant's face—we think he nailed it. Much like the male elephant. ZING!

We love that the sculptor made the male elephant's trunk wave in the air (like he just don't care), as if to say, "Wooo-fuckin'-hoo! Who's your daddy!" Meanwhile, his woman looks like she's just waiting for it to be over so she can roll over and watch *Seinfeld*. Animals: so like us.

ALL THAT GLITTERS IS CRAP

JEWELRY NO ONE SANE WOULD WEAR

The right accessories can make or break an outfit, so why settle for any boring old jewelry when you could have a stunning piece of crap instead? Earrings made out of animal droppings? Can do. A tongue ring featuring your favorite deity? *Amen.* A magic ring that will make your booty bumpin'? eBay is your place!

These items may not earn you any compliments, but they'll definitely get you some attention . . . and fewer invitations to cocktail parties and progressive dinners. That's not necessarily a bad thing, though.

12

CREMATION KEEPSAKE MEMORIAL BULLET KEYCHAIN URN

LOCATION: Roseburg, OR

COST: $4.99 + shipping

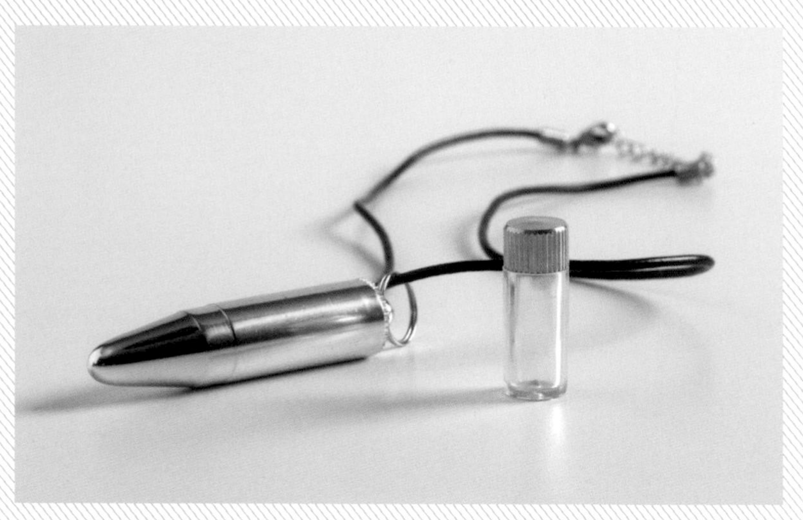

DESCRIPTION:

This auction is for one Bullet Cremation Keepsake Memorial Keychain Urn. This mini urn is discreet, sturdy, and secure, measures 2" tall (comes with a small clear vial inside to hold a small amount of your loved one) and is light and strong enough to carry them with you always. Can be used on a keyring or a necklace.

We don't know about you, but we often catch ourselves wishing we had charred bits of our dead loved ones to carry around with us everywhere we go. In a bullet. On a necklace.

Our wish just came true with this Cremation Keepsake Memorial Bullet Keychain Urn, an item that could really use a few more qualifiers in its name, no? This one's a bit vague.

Now, we know what you're thinking: wearing a bullet stuffed with human remains seems a bit—what's the word? Oh yeah—*insane*. But it's actually a powerful statement, one that says, "Don't fuck with me. I'm wearing what's left of the last guy who fucked with me." The bullet merely adds to the unspoken threat. It's not a real bullet, of course, but they won't know that.

The secret vial inside is the best part of this unlikely contraption, but even that seems like a better place to hide drugs than to tote Gramps around. But then, Gramps stayed pretty sauced before he died, so a snort of him would probably give you a sweeeeet buzz. We have no cremains of our own, so we contacted the seller to see if she could help.

↗ Dear Jack Ash,

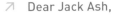

LOVE the Cremation Keepsake Memorial Bullet Keychain Necklace Secret Storage Thingamajobber That Holds Dead People's Ashes! What a clever idea. I want to buy it, but I don't have any cremains of my own. Do you have any spares you could give me? I don't care who it is as long as they weren't Republican.

S. Finkter

crickets

13

JESUS LOGO TONGUE BARBELL RING

LOCATION: West Palm Beach, FL

COST: $4.99

DESCRIPTION:

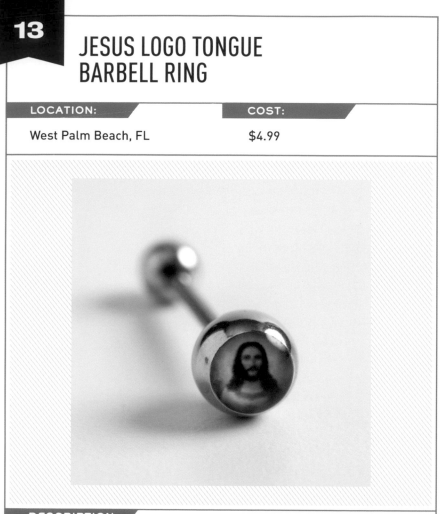

This is a top quality logo tongue ring. The picture inlay logo is crisp and well sealed, designed to last a lifetime. The barbell on this tongue ring is crafted from 316 lvm surgical grade stainless steel for your protection. Barbell Size: 14 Gauge Barbell. Length: ⅝"

As far as we know, excluding certain religious or cultural rationales, there are only a few reasons to pierce one's tongue in today's day and age:

1. To increase sensation while giving oral sex.
2. To be different from everyone else.
3. To annoy your parents.

Seeing as how this tongue ring has Jesus Christ on it, the question that begs to be answered is, "*Who* would Jesus do?" We like to think that wearing a Jesus tongue barbell may be kind of like having a tiny Jesus sitting in your mouth, offering guidance as only He can. Maybe He cleans up your potty mouth by editing some of the more profane expressions in your repertoire; instead of blurting out "Cocksucker!" at the moron who cut you off in traffic, you find yourself shouting "Cornhusker!" instead. You stub your toe and mutter a benign, "Shoot! Motherhugger!" instead of a more colorful expletive. The Jesus Filter could come in pretty handy.

Dieting? The Jesus tongue ring can help you with that, too. We can just see Jesus lounging on your tongue, propped up on one elbow with his legs crossed at the ankles, surveying all that passes your lips and giving His holy opinion about everything: "Ham again? Really? You're killin' me here! Ever heard of a vegetable? You know, those green things that are good for you? And who do I have to heal to get some wine up in here?"

Considering some of the nasty things people do with their mouths, who in their right mind would want the Son of God on their tongue? We've seen enough porn to know the score; some people are filthy heathens who will put just about anything in their pie holes. You really think Jesus wants to be involved in your little Catholic schoolgirl threesome fantasy? Hell no! Dude's got better things to do. We're sure you can find some other way to annoy the parental units. We hear Hooters is hiring.

14

REAL MOOSE POOP EARRINGS

LOCATION: Myrtle Beach, SC

COST: $10.99

DESCRIPTION:

Genuine moose poop nuggets, a product of Maine here in the US. Now you know what those folks do during those long New England winters! Bonkers, that's what, collecting moose droppings, drying them, coating them in polyurethane. I assure you there's NO smell. Nuggets are lightweight and average 1" long. GOLD tone hypoallergenic French wires.

When we started writing this book we had no idea that we'd *literally* be purchasing crap on eBay, but here we are. The seller insists that these earrings are great conversation-starters, but those don't sound like any conversations we'd like to have.

Picture it: you're at a cocktail party enjoying some lovely hors d'oeuvres when someone says, "Like my earrings? They're made out of moose shit." Classy! Good taste aside, we had a hard time imagining a huge animal like a moose producing teeny little poop pellets. Better email the seller.

↗ Dear Poo Peddler,

Is that really moose poop? Why is it so small? Seems like an animal that size could squeeze out more impressive turdage than this.

S. Finkter

↗ Dear S. Finkter,

Yes, it's real. Even deer poop is only the size of rabbit poop.

Poo Peddler

Wow. How can that be? It can't just be diet-related, because we have a friend who's a vegetarian and his giant logs are legendary. One more quick question.

↗ Dear Poo Peddler,

Thanks for the info. Do you ever do custom jewelry? I love my dog; any chance I could send you some of his turds and you could make me some earrings out of it? I think that would add sentimental value.

S. Finkter

Should we have mentioned that our dog is a Great Dane?

↗ Dear S. Finkter,

No, sorry. We do not do the moose poop prep. But moose and deer poop are already small and does not smell and is easily dried.

Poo Peddler

Well, darn. Oh well, we bought the earrings anyway. We're sure our mother-in-law, who is a huge animal lover, will adore them.

15

BELT BUCKLE: "EAT CHEESE OR DIE"

LOCATION: Taylor, MI

COST: $12.95

DESCRIPTION:

This is a beautifully detailed and BIG American-made belt buckle (5⅜" × 4⅛" Will fit up to a 1¾" belt) featuring motorcycles, a bearded biker, swooping eagle, bike-chain borders, stars, and the words "EAT CHEESE OR DIE" on the bottom. The back of the buckle contains the following script: "Jammin' in the wind on a long, straight stretch; kickin' it in the ass comin' out of a tight curve; or maybe just a slow cruise on a balmy night . . . it's a feeling you can only get on two wheels and there's nothin' else like it in the world."

When we think of bikers, we think of Harley-riding, chain-smoking, leather-wearing, metal-studded, tattooed, hairy-faced tough guys. We think of fat guys wearing tank tops that say stuff like, "If you can read this, the bitch fell off" on the back. We think of B.O. and Skoal. One thing we've never associated with bikers in any way, shape, or form is cheese . . . until we saw this fantastic biker belt buckle.

"Eat Cheese or Die" just doesn't seem fair—what about lactose-intolerant bikers? For them, it's more like "Eat Cheese AND Die," or if not die, then at least spend some uncomfortable hours on the john while their ass vomits sewage and they curse the horrible stroke of fate that left them unable to enjoy delicious dairy products.

For these poor bastards, "Eat Cheese or Die" sounds like a threat. We can just see a burly biker waving his buddies over to the side of the road. "Hang on guys," he'd grumble around a mouthful of chaw, "I ate some of that goddamn queso dip back there. Gotta cut some more logs." Poor sucker. It has to be hard to have the runs with 650 pounds of vibrating metal between your legs.

Then there's the matter of the lovely poem etched into the back. Who knew that burly bikers could be so sentimental? Thanks to this magnificent belt buckle, we're pretty sure that under their gruff exteriors lie the hearts of poets and philosophers. Cheese-loving poets and philosophers, that is.

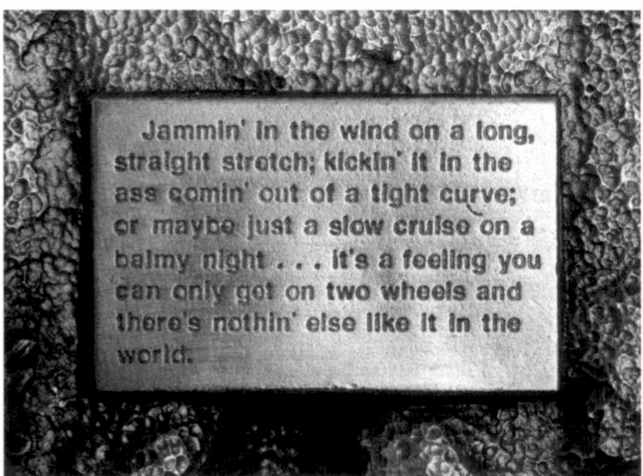
Jammin' in the wind on a long, straight stretch; kickin' it in the ass comin' out of a tight curve; or maybe just a slow cruise on a balmy night . . . it's a feeling you can only get on two wheels and there's nothin' else like it in the world.

16

BOOTY ENHANCER SPELL RING

LOCATION:	COST:
Columbus, IN	$17.95

DESCRIPTION:

REAL AUSTRIAN CRYSTAL RING! THIS AUCTION IS FOR A VOODOO "BABY GOT BACK!" BOOTY SPELL RING! A WHITE MAGIC BUTT & THIGH ENHANCEMENT SPELL FOR MEN OR WOMEN. IMPROVES THE BOOTY GIVING A NICE ROUND BUBBLE BUTT, TIGHTENS LOOSE SKIN, REDUCES FAT OR CELLULITE, ENHANCES THE BOOTY IN AREAS YOU MAY NEED IT MOST.

Tell the truth. Does this ring make our butts look big? Many women hate their asses, a fact which necessitates a huge market for everything from fake booty padding and surgical implants to umpteen million *Buns of Steel* videos, but does anyone out there honestly think that wearing a bewitched ring is going to give them a juicy J-Lo butt?

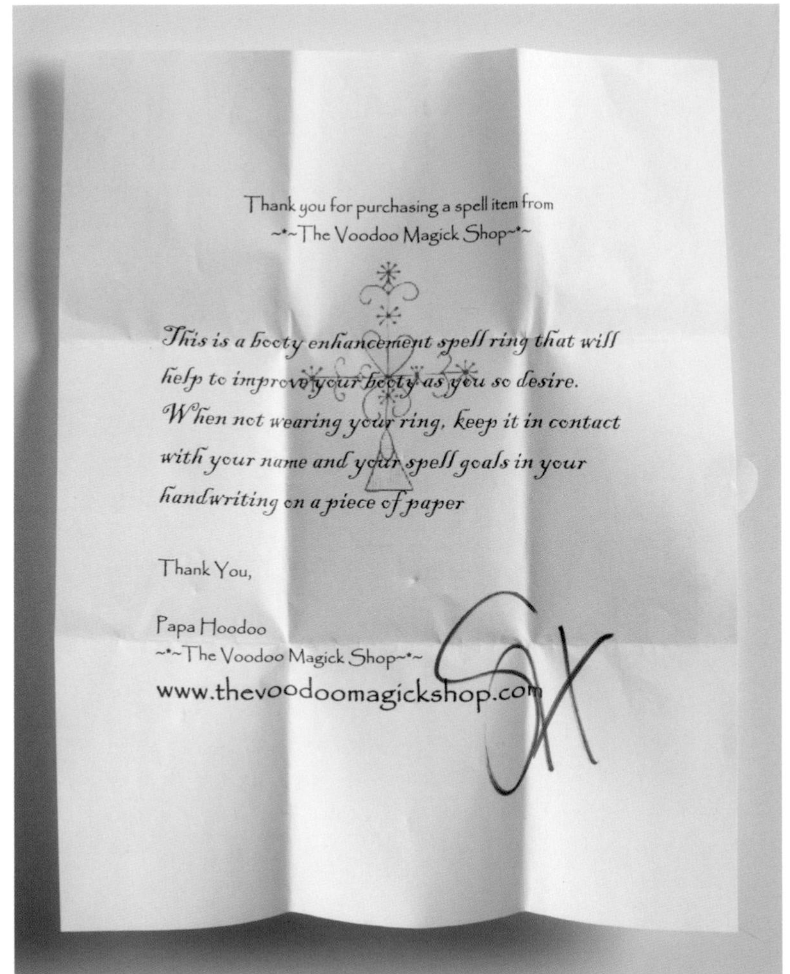

Thank you for purchasing a spell item from
~*~The Voodoo Magick Shop~*~

This is a booty enhancement spell ring that will help to improve your booty as you so desire. When not wearing your ring, keep it in contact with your name and your spell goals in your handwriting on a piece of paper

Thank You,

Papa Hoodoo
~*~The Voodoo Magick Shop~*~
www.thevoodoomagickshop.com

Since voodoo is not what you would call an exact science, we kept picturing it like a scene from a Stephen King book; the spell starts off working great, but before long you've got elephantiasis of the ass and you have to buy an extra seat for it on Southwest Air. Anyone who has ever spent a flight from Fresno to Toledo sitting next to a giant ass can tell you that it's no fun. No fun at all.

This description points out that the spell works for both men and women, yet we've never met a dude who wants a bigger backside. We went ahead and *assed* the seller a few questions. It *tuchus* a while to reach him, and we ended up *butt*ing heads just a little bit, but it was worth it. We hate to *ass*ume anything.

↗ Dear Seymour Butts,

My husband likes big butts, but mine is flat as a pancake. I need this ring. How does the spell work?

S. Finkter

↗ Dear S. Finkter,

Our voodoo priestess casts a powerful spell on the ring so your butt looks more toned and round. When you're not wearing the ring you should keep it next to a piece of paper with your name on it and it will still work.

Seymour Butts

↗ Dear Seymour Butts,

Great! Will it do anything to cure my ass pimples?

S. Finkter

↗ Dear S. Finkter,

I'm not sure if it will help with acne, but I do have other spells for that problem so please look at my other auctions!

Seymour Butts

One thing we know for sure is that if this booty spell *really* worked, the seller should look pretty phenomenal. Think about it; if you could conjure spells to cure your various body flaws, wouldn't you look incredible? We would. That is, if we needed spells, which we totally don't. Nope. Uh uh, no way. **whistling**

But we're wearing the ring, just in case.

17

VINTAGE HUMPING ARMADILLOS PIN

LOCATION:

Colony, OK

COST:

$4.99

DESCRIPTION:

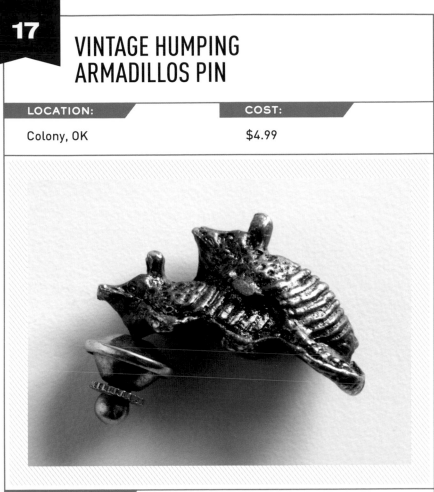

This bid is for a vintage tie tack pin or hat pin that is silver color metal and about 1¼ inches long. It is a pair of Armadillos "breeding." A nice unusual collectible for armadillo lovers, this will be shipped well packaged in bubble wrap and with delivery confirmation and postal tracking number.

Prior to writing this book, we really didn't know much about armadillos, so when we spotted this unusual metal pin of two armadillos doing it doggy-style (armadillo-style?) we were intrigued. Are armadillos known for being particularly amorous?

Actually, no, they're not. Armadillos are generally loners, like one-man wolf packs, except for once a year when they seek out other armadillos to make the beast with two hard backs and repopulate their kind. Makes you wonder if the she-madillo ever gets tired of waiting for that once-a-year booty call from the he-madillo.

For the life of us, we could not figure out who would ever want to create or wear a mating armadillo pin. We're sure some people do *like* these weird little rodents, but even if you're a certifiable armadillo fanatic, why get a pin of them doing the nasty?

Since we're modern writers, we did the modern thing and Googled armadillos to find out what might be so intriguing about their mating rituals that it would justify the creation, sale, and purchase of a humping armadillo pin. That's how we wound up on YouTube watching two armadillos in a zoo going at it while a giggling family of tourists videotaped it, an image that will forever be seared into our brains.

This book has truly taken us to some odd places on the Web; we only hope that you appreciate our efforts, because what we've seen cannot be unseen.

18

VULVA/CLITORIS SILVER PENDANT

LOCATION:

USA

COST:

$19.99

DESCRIPTION:

You are buying a new solid silver, very unique vagina-clitoris charm pendant. This is not silver plated, this is a solid sterling silver pendant 925K stamp on it. This pendant looks much better in person. The ring's diameter is ¼ inch or 5 mm. With the ring on, the overall length is about 1½ inches or 4 cm. This eye-catching and amazingly crafted pendant will bring you new erotic moods. It will be a great gift for you or your lover.

Hey look! It's a dainty silver pendant in the shape of your business. Your *lady* business. Just what you've always wanted. Even though this pendant is actually quite tiny, all of the nooks and crannies of your average pink taco are represented. Little man in a boat? Check. Gaping labia? Check. Itty bitty taint? Representin'!

The silver pendant may be small, but like all coochies, it has a certain magical *je ne sais quoi*. You can't deny the magic of female genitalia—women throughout the ages have whipped their men into submission with just the promise of a *glimpse* of their goodies, after all. How else would we get men to mow the lawn or take out the trash if it weren't for the power of the almighty kitty?

That, my friends, is the magic of the love muffin. Never underestimate its power. But what's the deal with wearing vajewelry? The listing says this is a great gift for your lover, but who would give this thing to anyone they want to continue fucking? Does anyone *really* want to wear a tiny silver hoo-ha around their neck?

It almost seems like the kind of thing a jealous girlfriend might give her man. We're thinking of Glenn Close in *Fatal Attraction* presenting poor Michael Douglas with this craptastic trinket of her insanity. "You'd better wear this graven image of my twat to stave off the advances of other, less crazy women, Dan. Or the bunny gets it!"

We're not saying you'd have to be nuttier than squirrel poop to wear a Sterling Silver Vulva Pendant, but it wouldn't hurt.

YOU WEAR THAT CRAP IN PUBLIC?

APPAREL FOR THE BLIND OR DEEPLY DISTURBED

We are constantly amazed by some of the outfits that people will wear while out and about. Just a simple trip to the mall proves to be a freaky fashion show: teenagers wearing flannel pajama pants; grandmothers in t-shirts that say inappropriate things like "GILF" or "Who needs a man? I have batteries"; and denim leggings (jeggings?) . . . on men.

However, all of those undignified wardrobe choices pale in comparison with the crazy clothing and accessories that we found on eBay. It's hard to believe that anyone would be caught dead in this stuff, but hey, to each his own. We don't judge. Much.

19

"SPANK MY MONKEY" SEQUINED THONG

LOCATION: Dallas, TX

COST: $9.99

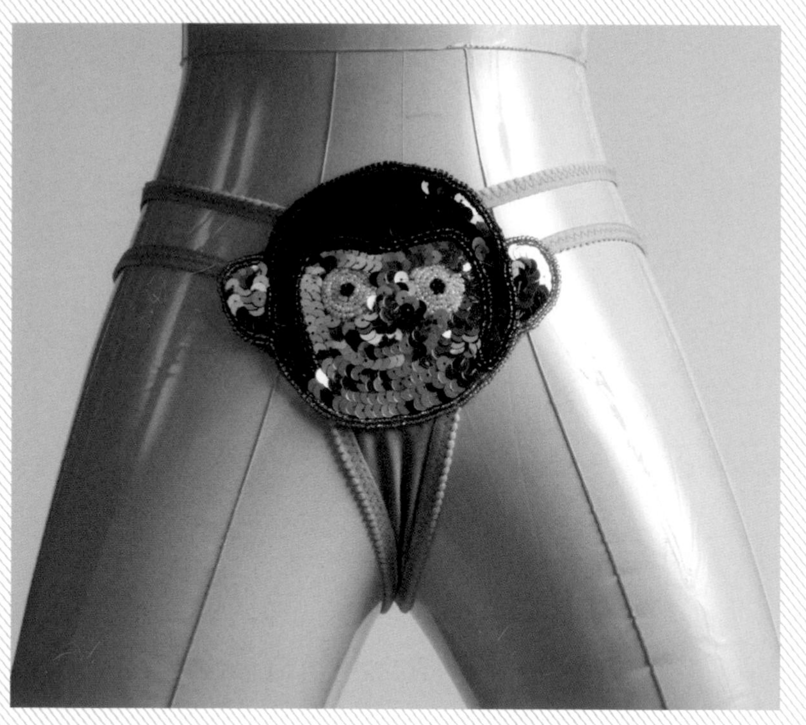

DESCRIPTION:

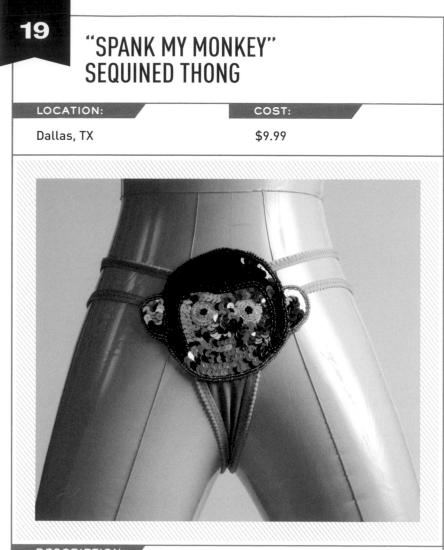

What a dirty little boy! This naughty thong depicts a monkey face adorned in sequins and glass beads. Double straps on the sides. Fun! One size fits all. Gold/sequins.

We're all used to getting a little shock when we first glimpse what someone is packing down under. Maybe it's a giant bush, a particularly large or small unit, or just a creative wax job. What you're never expecting, however, is a pair of beaded googly eyes peering back at you.

Wearing this "one-size-fits-all" (yeah right) spangly thong, ladies will be sure to get a reaction from their men, no doubt about that. Problem is he'll most likely burst into either laughter or tears, and both of those reactions are mood-killers, plain and simple. This itty bitty number is covered in sequins in the form of a monkey face peering out from between your legs, and nothing says "do me" like a sparkly monkey face on your cooch.

We suppose it makes sense; monkeys like bananas, after all. Plus, if there's one thing the exotic dancing industry has taught us, it's that men are like fish: dangle something that glimmers in front of them and they will open their mouths and bite at it without thinking about the consequences.

Still, something tells us that wearing a monkey thong is the equivalent of wearing a bacon bra. It's intriguing and comical, but not exactly sexy. Do your beaver a favor: skip the primate section of the lingerie store.

20

MEN'S DISCO SHOES: 3-INCH PLATFORM HEEL WITH GOLDFISH

LOCATION:	COST:
Marina Del Rey, CA	$52

DESCRIPTION:

3" Heel Platform Men's Disco Shoes with Goldfish in Heel (Men's Sizes)

Size: 8. COLOR: Silver with Clear Heel

The good news: we found Nemo! The bad news: he didn't make it. Not only are these sparkly platform shoes for *men*, but they've also got a miniature aquarium in the heels!

↗ Dear Huggy Bear,

I'm concerned about the fish in my heels—they appear to be dead. Was I supposed to feed them or something?

S. Finkter

Dear S. Finkter,

The goldfish in your shoes are not real. They're made of plastic.

Huggy Bear

Whew!

↗ Dear Huggy Bear,

Well, how do I replace them with live fish?

S. Finkter

↗ Dear S. Finkter,

You don't.

Huggy Bear

Well, okay then. We got kind of used to having a little goldfish floating belly-up in our heels, but people did stare when we wore them out in public. Of course, it's entirely possible that they were staring because we were walking around the grocery store wearing sparkly iridescent platform pimp shoes that weigh about three pounds apiece, but we can't be sure about that.

What, a pimp can't buy an eggplant?

21

NYLON STOCKING CHANGE PURSE

LOCATION:

Alkol (Alcohol?), WV

COST:

$4.99

DESCRIPTION:

This is a change purse made with a nylon stocking. First one I ever saw. Measures 40".

This makes sense: a change purse made from a woman's stocking, because stockings are so durable. It takes a lot to make them run—a glance, or the stiff breeze from a gnat's wing. Naturally, then, a stocking makes the perfect place to keep piles of heavy metal change, especially a forty-inch (count 'em!) stocking that once belonged to Paul Bunyan's wife.

Cary's wife has a Southernism she likes to use whenever Cary, the world's worst handyman, uses duct tape or staples to "fix" an appliance or "hang" a ceiling fan. The expression is, "That will last about as long as Pat stayed in the Army," and it means not very long. Whoever Pat was—no one seems to know—we're sure he would be thrilled to know that his extraordinarily brief military career is now being used as a metaphor for anything that is destined to fail, and quickly. Like a change purse made from a stocking.

That's too bad, because it would probably hold about $977* in quarters alone, except it would be so heavy you'd have to drag the lumpy engorged beast behind you, which would look like you were taking the world's largest turd for a walk. Unless you got smart, like that guy in Africa who had elephantiasis of the balls, and finally invested in a wheelbarrow to ease your load.

*estimated

22

BOOB SCARF

LOCATION:

Colorado, USA

COST:

$24

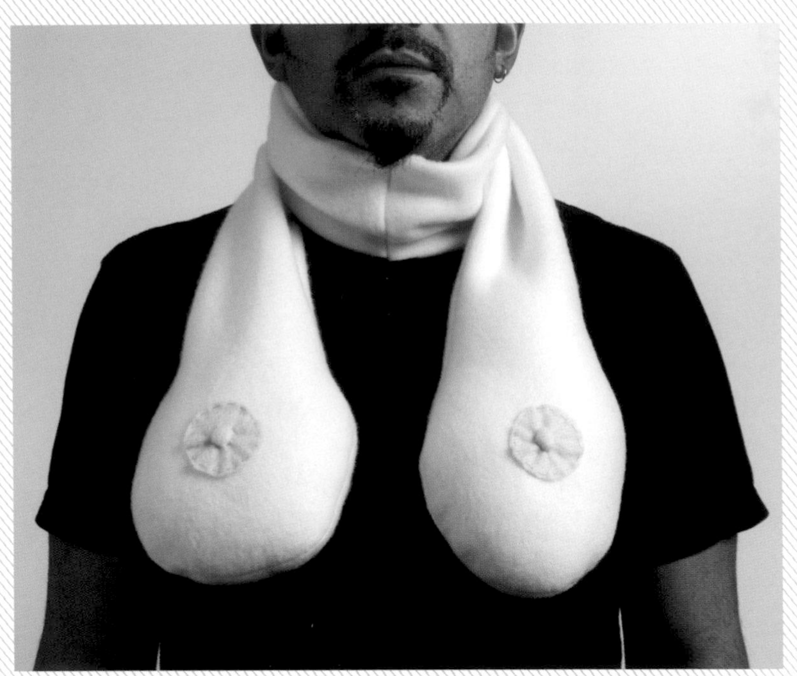

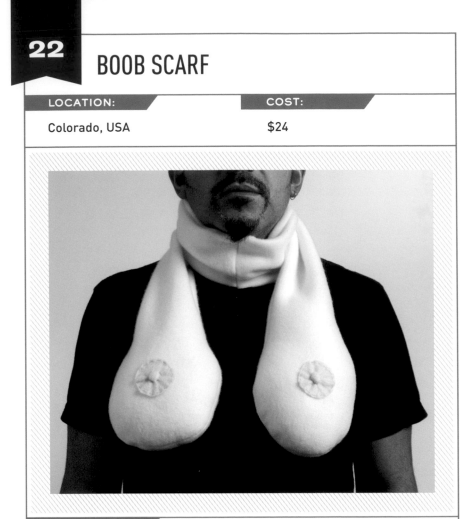

DESCRIPTION:

Soft & squishy . . . fun to squeeze! With PINK or TAN nipples. Excellent conversation piece, sure to bring giggles & grins! Great for bachelor parties, gag gifts, or for everyday fun!! Made from baby soft fleece, felt, & extra squishy batting.

When we first spotted this fleece scarf with pendulous ta-tas, we knew we had to have it. After all, scarves are so fashionable, and we are nothing if not cutting edge. We had to laugh imagining Juanita the underpaid Mexican seamstress slaving over a sewing machine to create these jubblies for those oddball Americans, but once we contacted the seller, we found that these scarves are not mass-produced at all; each one of them is lovingly hand-crafted by a soccer mom in Colorado.

The scarves were listed for thirty-five dollars or best offer, so we haggled her down to her breaking point of twenty-four dollars, at which point she said: "I typically don't sell these for less than twenty-five dollars because of the cost of the fleece. If you'd like to purchase one just let me know because I would love to make one for you!!!!!"

All of those exclamation points and the fact that she is clearly dying to make one *just for us* kind of got us right here.**tapping heart** We gladly paid our twenty-four dollars and were rewarded with a beautifully crafted scarf with two monstrous squishy boobs dangling from the ends.

Upon closer examination it was clear that Soccer Mom had personally hand-stitched the pink nipples on, giving it a certain Tara Reid "Frankentit" boob-job quality. We don't mind, though—we can take off our scarf whenever we want. Poor Tara isn't so lucky.

The boobs are also oddly squished, as if they'd been caught in a mammogram machine for about three hours and had yet to spring back to shape. The most fun part about wearing this scarf is when we get to roll our eyes at people who stare at our fleecy bosom and say, "Um, hello? Eyes up *here*, please!" That's just good fun. After all, isn't confusing strangers what the Boob Scarf is all about?

23

MEN'S RED ELEPHANT POUCH

LOCATION:

Marlton, NJ

COST:

$2.99

DESCRIPTION:

Nylon red elephant men's pouch with hollow trunk for fun. One size fits all. Spice up your night. Great fun for bachelorette parties.

Elephant trunk thong underwear. Of course! What, you don't have a pair? Oh well, they aren't for everyone, Pee Wee.

We don't mean to be rude; we're sure you all have talented penises that leave all the girls screaming for more. It's just that—well, how do we say this delicately? That's a pretty big trunk, and unless your resumé says "Adult Film Star" somewhere on it, we seriously doubt most of you are up to the challenge.

The average dong may fill half of this thing, two-thirds if it's lucky. Some won't even make a dent in it, bless their wee little hearts. The result will be more sad platypus than elephant, and that's not really the look you were going for, is it?

Don't worry, though: you're better off without these, trust us. For one, elephants love nuts, which keeps us on high alert whenever we wear these. Elephants also remember everything, including things we've forgotten. Things we might have done with our crotch, for example. While we were drunk. With one or two, um, *ample* young women we managed to sneak out of the house before our roommates woke up and saw them. (Hence the saying, "She's not ugly if no one sees her.")

The elephant pouch saw her. It knows all of our dirty secrets. That's why we're nice to it. The pouch has us by the balls, in more ways than one.

24

USED SEXY MEN'S BEIGE SOCKS

LOCATION:	COST:
New York, NY	$6.50

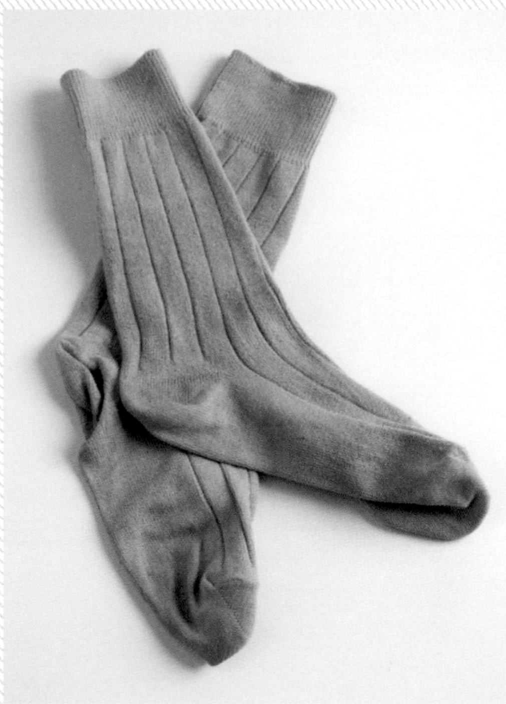

DESCRIPTION:

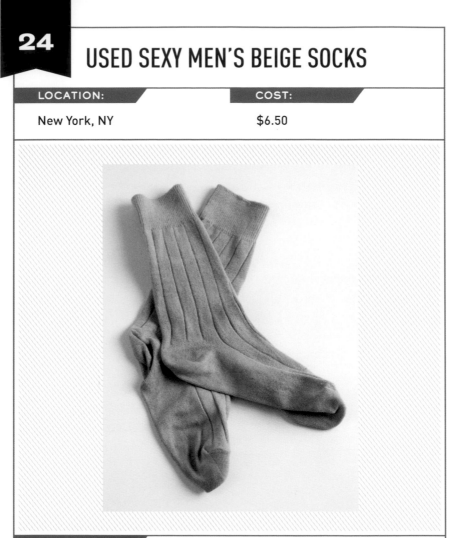

Used beige that I have used during the summer—very sexy socks, great to show off. Kick your shoes off and look like a million bucks. Will be shipped washed and clean as per eBay rules and manufacturers' standards. I wear these for a couple of days and they feel great. They look great on my feet too, seem to get lots of attention.

Here at CIBOE headquarters, we see a lot of freaky items, yet none of the wacky, oddball, and often disgusting crap we bought for this book grossed us out as much as this simple pair of men's socks.

This entrepreneurial chump is not the first to list his dirty socks online. Just type "used socks" into your eBay search bar and you'll be rewarded with about *fifteen pages* of people trying to hock their used, stinky, germ-ridden socks. Every kind of sock is represented, all modeled by their current owners, all sharing just one frightening attribute: they're filthy and smell bad. And that's their *allure*.

We saw college frat boys advertising their tattered sweat socks, a dancer displaying her dainty ankle socks, and a professional weightlifter showing off his visibly stained and holey socks. We saw people fighting over forty-five-dollar soiled socks. All sellers claimed that their socks are the stinkiest (and therefore sexiest) of them all.

It was hard to select just one pair of socks to bid on, but we settled on these because the seller said they'd get us lots of attention, and hey, we love attention. Just want to clarify a few things:

↗ Dear Swampfoot,

These are great, but I would prefer them unwashed. Can you do that?

S. Finkter

↗ Dear S. Finkter,

Yea, of course, that's how I send most socks.

Swampfoot

Ah, so that part about washing them according to eBay's standards was all a ruse to keep The Man off his back. We can dig it. One more question.

↗ Dear Swampfoot,

Great! How would you describe their smell?

S. Finkter

↗ Dear S. Finkter,

Well, depends how long I wear them for. Foot smells nice, sweaty, and smelly.

Swampfoot

If you're anything like us, this is the point of the conversation where you discovered a bit of upchuck in your mouth. Still, it made us wonder if there's an eBay market for soiled kids' underwear, because we could make a mint.

CRAP FROM THE TOY CHEST

EVEN KIDS KNOW CRAP WHEN THEY SEE IT

Just because kids can entertain themselves with an empty cardboard box and a dirt clod doesn't mean they don't love great interactive toys. In this chapter, you won't find any great interactive toys, though, just a bunch of crap that will give your poor offspring chronic nightmares and earn them a lunchtime beat-down should they take any of it to school. These toys were all surely donated to charity at some point, but no doubt returned the next day, because even a homeless blind orphan would rather play with his own excrement than a Vanilla Ice doll or a lice plush.

Kids are lots of things, but stupid isn't one of them. They can smell crap from a mile away.

25

HAUNTED DOLL SINGS "TWINKLE, TWINKLE"

LOCATION:	COST:
Round Rock, TX	$4.99 + shipping

DESCRIPTION:

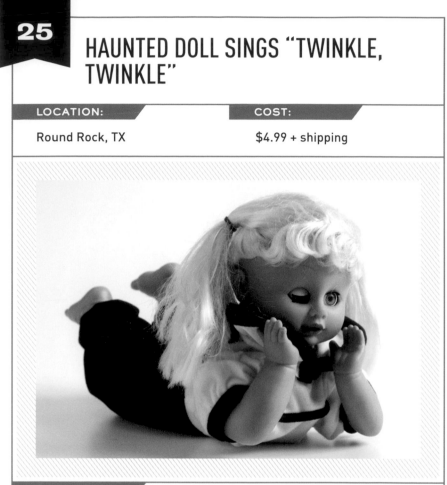

This doll sings "Twinkle Twinkle Little Star" (loudly) while bobbing her head back and forth and kicking her legs. She is possessed by a sweet spirit of a little girl named Angel. She is lying down on her stomach (this is her fixed position . . . she can't do any other pose). She has blonde hair in ponytails and her eyes open and close. She is approximately 14 inches long. There is an on/off switch and a button to push on her back to make her sing. The battery compartment is also on her back (uses 3 AA batteries, sorry not included).

This isn't your ordinary funked-up-looking doll. The seller claims that this doll is possessed by the spirit of a child named Angel whose tragic backstory is filled with hunger, despair, and jingle-singing. However, now that Angel's soul has moved on to a happier plane of being, she inhabits the doll and brings a sweet, mirthful vibe to your home. She also likes to move objects around and whisper sweet nothings into your ear while you sleep.

No, that's not creepy at all. We've seen the *Chucky* movies. We know how this story ends, thanks. You awake in the middle of the night to find Angel hovering over you, crazy-eyed and wielding a cleaver, ready to separate your face from your head. No thanks.

Perhaps we'd be interested if she helped around the house a little—tidied up the yard or did the laundry, for instance. But if she's just going to sit there and talk and move our stuff without asking, forget it. We have *real* kids for that.

26

DEAD BODY ACTION FIGURE ON GURNEY

LOCATION:

Macon, GA

COST:

$15.99

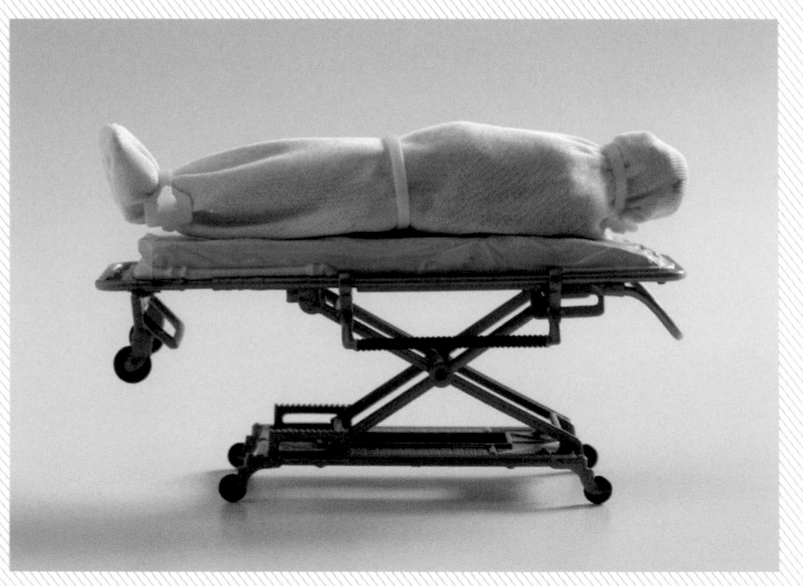

DESCRIPTION:

Christmas is just around the corner! GURNEY AND BODY ARE BRAND NEW, COMPLETE WITH BODY WRAPPED IN A WHITE SHROUD. BOTH GURNEY AND BODY ARE APPROXIMATELY 2" WIDE and 6" LONG. The gurney goes up & down and is made of plastic. The side rails also swing up and down. All six wheels are molded plastic and do not roll. This gurney is intended for a desktop display. It's the perfect item for your miniature Doll House or Coroner Scene. It will fit inside a 1/12 scale Hearse.

Dead body action figure. Of course—because corpses are so active. That's why we call them *stiffs*—because they move so much.

↗ Dear Guy Selling Creepy Toys,

Nice dead guy, but how exactly is this an "action" figure? What does it do besides lie there? I don't think decomposing really counts. Too bad the gurney doesn't roll. That might count.

S. Finkter

↗ Dear S. Finkter,

It is an expression. The figure does not do anything.

Guy Selling Creepy Toys

↗ Dear Guy Selling Creepy Toys,

Okay then. Maybe you should call it an "INaction figure." That would be a more accurate expression. Or "plastic statue." That's a good expression, too.

S. Finkter

No answer. Did we offend? It's fine—no toy is perfect. Kids will still love adding a corpse to their figure collection. They can pretend it's one of Batman's parents, or Spiderman's Uncle Ben, or Obi-Wan Kenobi after Darth Vader dissects him with a light saber.

Or they can include it in a coroner scene, as the seller suggests, because you know how much kids love coroner scenes. Okay, not really. A few might, but they're the ones who grow up and keep heads in the freezer and make bracelets out of teeth and say things like, "It rubs the lotion on its skin or else it gets the hose again."

The figure would make a nice addition to Texting Barbie's Highway Slaughter Playset, though. You can pretend it's Earring Magic Ken, who was in the passenger seat reading *Star* when tragedy struck.

Since we are curious and morbid freaks, we had to unwrap the figure and see who was inside. You'll never guess who we found. That's right—R.E.M.'s Michael Stipe. With E.T.'s body. Michael Stipe, phone home!

27

GIANTMICROBES® HEAD LICE PLUSH

LOCATION:

Middleboro, MA

COST:

$7.95

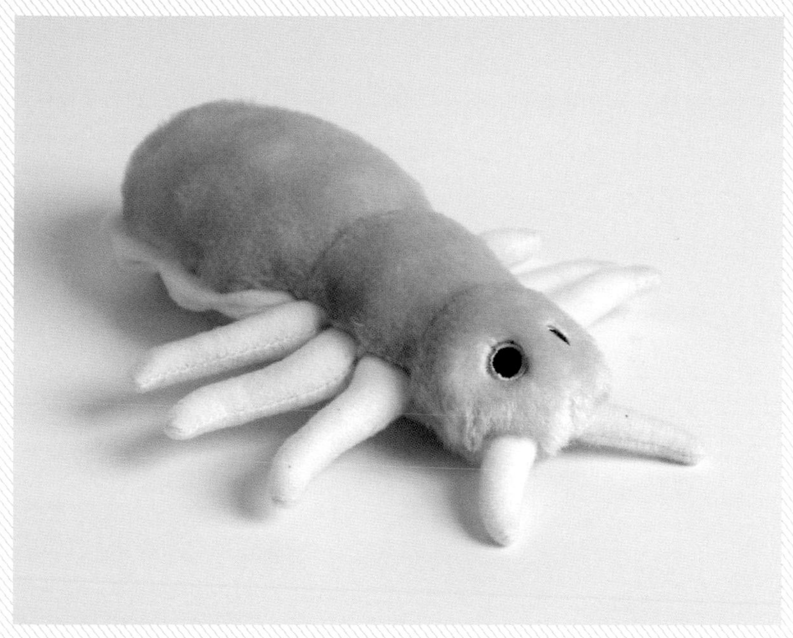

DESCRIPTION:

GIANTmicrobes® are stuffed animals that look like tiny microbes—only a million times actual size! They're humorous, educational, and fun! Each of our GIANTmicrobes® comes with an image and information about the real microbe it represents. GIANTmicrobes® are not only soft and lovable, they are extremely well made and durable. They make great learning tools, as well as amusing gifts for anyone with a sense of humor.

Attention parents! We've found the perfect cuddly toy for your kids. Next time your child comes home scratching his grimy little head, pull out one of these adorable stuffed head lice toys and make it a teaching moment! Once the kid starts snuggling his new pals, he's bound to feel a whole lot better about the fact that his hair is infested with thousands of swarming, microscopic, egg-laying vermin, and there's a really bad haircut in his future.

Better yet—and here's the best news in microbes since penicillin—there's a whole line of these cuddly little disease dolls for every member of your family, including Harriet Herpes, Elvis Coli, Sal Manella, Lydia Chlamydia, Ann Thrax, Gangrene Gene, and many, many, more!

Collect them all—they're cooler than Beanie Babies, and no one will fight you over them. In fact, these may be the perfect addition to that basket you're making up for an expectant mom. Throw a plush microbe into a baby shower gift and watch as the room goes silent as she unwraps it. There's nothing like welcoming someone to motherhood by reminding her that someday her little snotmonger will come home infested with head lice. Awww.

We know they're trying to teach kids about disease, but we're not sure putting a pair of freaky, bulging eyeballs on a disease is going to encourage kids to wash their hands. Most kids would still think boogers are gross even if they have a plush toy shaped like one. And they'd be right.

28

ROCKY BEST OF SERIES 1 FRANK STALLONE FIGURE

LOCATION:	COST:
Pennsylvania, USA	$6.95

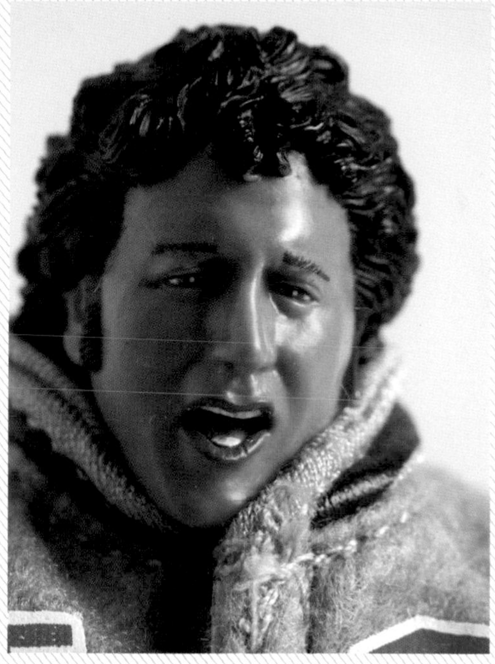

DESCRIPTION:

This Rocky figure is Frank Stallone and is part of the extremely rare Rocky Best of Series I figure collection by Jakks Pacific. This figure is very rare and is a must for any Rocky fan's figure collection. I just acquired an estate full of Rocky, Mr. T, and A-Team items so check back soon and often!

YOU: Who? Frank Stallone? Who's that?
US: Oh, c'mon, you remember Frank from the first *Rocky*, don'tcha? He played "Street Corner Singer" in that pivotal scene where he's, uh, singing and he's on the street corner? Then Rocky walks by and maybe says "Yo!" or something and gives him a nod? Okay, we don't remember him, either. This can't be a real action figure. eBay is full of pranksters and grifters.

↗ Dear Hoodafukk S. Frankstallone,

Is this a custom figure you made? I've seen *Rocky* many times and I don't remember this person in the movie.

S. Finkter

↗ Dear S. Finkter,

Not custom. Part of *Rocky* series as listing states. He is in the movie. Frank is Slyvester's [sic] brother and had a small role.

Hoodafukk S. Frankstallone

↗ Dear Hoodafukk S. Frankstallone,

Yeah, so small it doesn't exist. Doesn't matter, though, I like custom figures. I know the body is from a Richie Cunningham/*Happy Days* doll, but whose head is that? Will Ferrell? Ronald McDonald?

S. Finkter

↗ Dear S. Finkter,

As I said, it is part of the Rocky collection. You can believe it or not, I don't really care. Frank Stallone was in the movie.

Hoodafukk S. Frankstallone

↗ Dear Hoodafukk S. Frankstallone,

Okay, Frank. That's right: you are Frank Stallone. You can't fool me. You made this figure yourself so you could pretend to be in *Rocky* and make a few bucks on eBay, didn't you? Nice try, Frank, but no cigar.

S. Finkter

↗ Dear S. Finkter,

Fuck off, idiot.

Frank

See? We were right.

Show of hands—who wants to watch me pound my salami?

29

VINTAGE MENUDO CARDS 1983 WAX PACK

LOCATION:

Staten Island, NY

COST:

$0.99

DESCRIPTION:

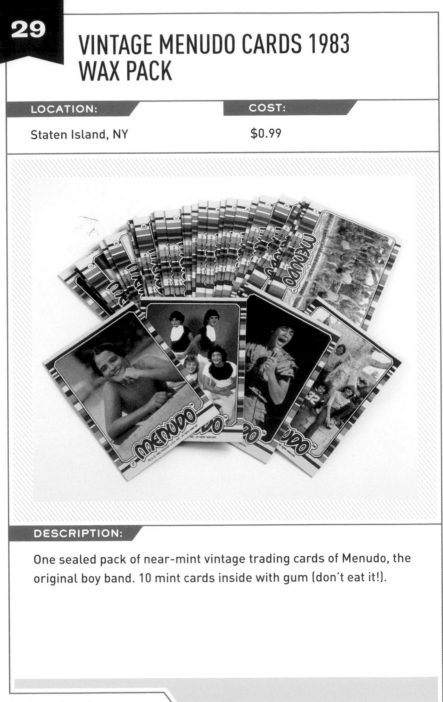

One sealed pack of near-mint vintage trading cards of Menudo, the original boy band. 10 mint cards inside with gum (don't eat it!).

You're probably too young to have heard of Menudo, so let us fill you in. Grab a beverage, because this is exciting stuff. Menudo was arguably the first boy band, long before New Edition, New Kids, Backstreet Boys, or any of those other lame posers who are so not cute at all. We say arguably because some consider The Jackson 5 a boy band, but Tito was at least thirty-seven when they recorded, so they don't count.

During their highly successful thirty-two-year reign as the prepubescent princes of Puerto Rican pop, Menudo had several radio hits, released forty albums, and boasted thirty-five different members, including Ricky Martin ("Livin' la Vida Loca"), Robby Rosa, Caleb Avilés, Roberto Clemente, Juan Valdez, Chita Rivera, Speedy Gonzales, Julio Iglesias, Rita Moreno, Che Guevara, Pancho Villa, and Juan Ponce de Léon.

One reason for the high turnover in the band is that boys must leave the group when they turn sixteen, as this is the age when young men typically begin to resist wearing costumes made from discarded linens and posing for shirtless photographs that clearly appeal more to pedophiles than to teenage girls.

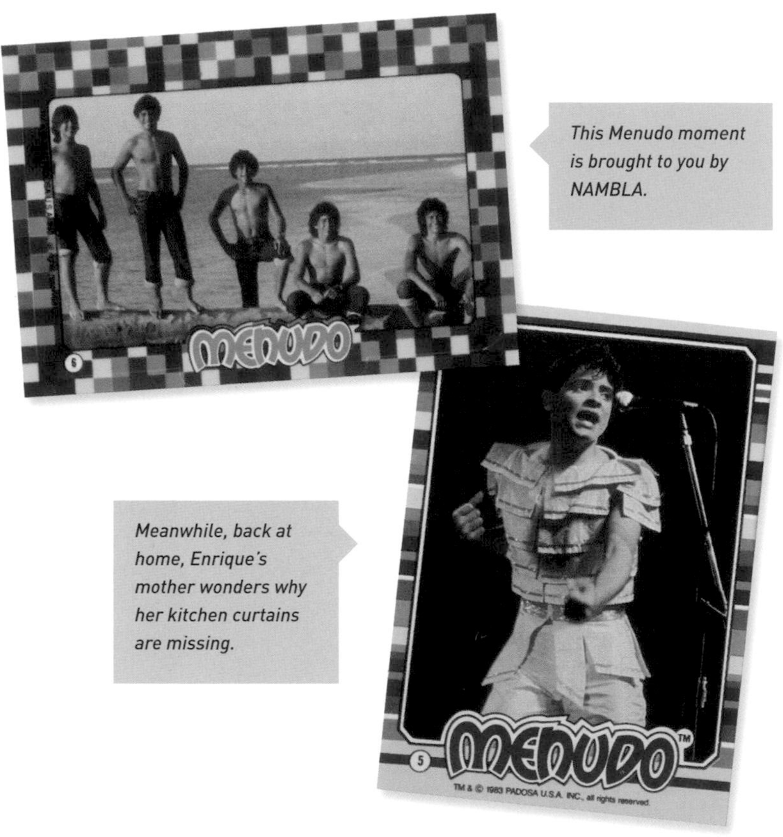

This Menudo moment is brought to you by NAMBLA.

Meanwhile, back at home, Enrique's mother wonders why her kitchen curtains are missing.

30

VANILLA ICE DOLL

LOCATION: Teaneck, NJ

COST: $10.99

DESCRIPTION:

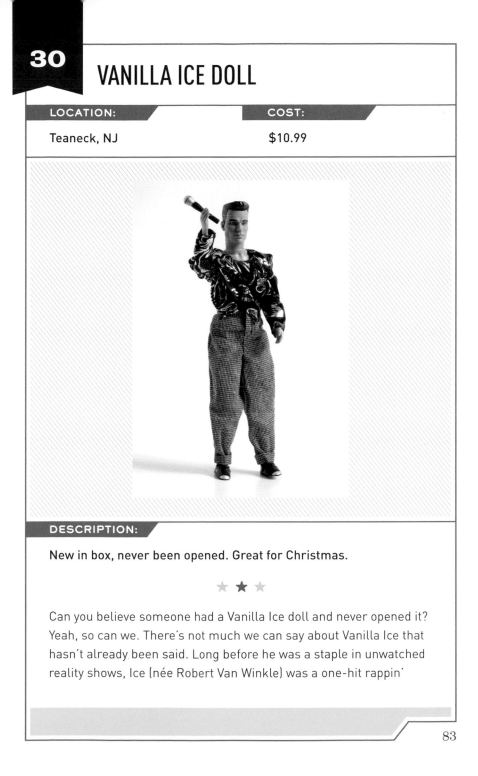

New in box, never been opened. Great for Christmas.

Can you believe someone had a Vanilla Ice doll and never opened it? Yeah, so can we. There's not much we can say about Vanilla Ice that hasn't already been said. Long before he was a staple in unwatched reality shows, Ice (née Robert Van Winkle) was a one-hit rappin'

wonder in the early nineties, the original wanksta (honky trying to be gangsta), and, briefly, a movie actor. By briefly we mean one movie, which is as brief a career as any actor can have. If you ever saw his movie, *Cool as Ice*, you'll agree that this is not always a bad thing.

But then, Vanilla Ice isn't the only one-hit wonder who ever recorded a song that makes you want to shoot yourself in the face when you hear it (Willow Smith, anyone?), or the only actor we ever saw who had no business being on a movie screen ('sup, Cindy Crawford), so we'll give the guy a pass.

His "action figure," however, is a different animal entirely. This thing is totally tubular, and perfect for our post-ironic washed-up celebrity doll-and-action-figure collection, which includes M.C. Hammer, Potsie from *Happy Days*, Farrah Fawcett-Majors with Arctic Blast Nipples™, Dennis Rodman in a wedding dress, Mayim Bialik as Blossom in *Good Touch, Bad Touch: A Very Special Blossom*, Spiro Agnew, and Frank Stallone in *Rocky*. Even though Frank Stallone wasn't in *Rocky*, the liar.

COLLECTIBLE CRAP

PERFECT FOR YOUR CRAP COLLECTION

Just when you thought your grandmother's chipped tea cup collection was weird, something comes along to remind you of one simple fact: truly strange people collect truly strange stuff. In this chapter, you'll find all sorts of quirky, nasty, and downright bizarre items that are perfect for that connoisseur of crap in your life. Tell Grandma to make some room on her tea cup shelf, because we've got the perfect additions to her crap collection right here.

31

AMERICANA TRIBAL SALT AND PEPPER SHAKERS

LOCATION:	COST:
Upton, MA	$6.51

DESCRIPTION:

You are looking at an Old Vintage Black Americana Tribal Men Bust Set of Salt and Pepper Shakers. They are in Good vintage condition (in my opinion, NOT MINT). This is a pretty cool looking and colorful set! A GREAT set to add to any collection. Makes a GREAT gift. The pictures show the detail on the item nicely. All shakers listed are truly meant for collecting purposes!!! NOT INTENDED FOR USE!!

These salt and pepper shakers are for folks who like to season their food with a little Creepy As Fuck and Weird As Hell. The fact that the seller specified several times (in great detail) that we are NOT to use them as actual salt and pepper shakers under ANY circumstances speaks volumes. These are strictly for admiring—don't let them near your food unless you feel like dying from a rare form of lead poisoning.

Or maybe these things are cursed by some bizarre tiki gods, so if you use them to sprinkle seasoning on your food your head will shrink, your tongue will swell, and you'll rue the day you didn't respect the shaker seller's warning. We can't think of any other reason why this generic souvenir shouldn't be used for its intended purpose.

Aside from their mysterious uselessness, these things just look ridonkulous, kind of like they were created on craft day at the local rehabilitation home for the mentally challenged. We can picture an old dude in soiled Depends trying to focus his double vision enough to dab some paint on these shakers. Yes, there are eyes in the general area where eyes should be, but should they be so bulbous, cross-eyed, and googly?

We've done the whole "paint your own pottery" thing and made our own mistakes with a paintbrush and ceramics, but we never tried to sell our craptastic pottery, and we never created salt and pepper shakers that look like a couple of inbred twins who ride the short bus and have a collective IQ of eighty-seven.

One thing we do know for sure is that these would definitely not make an excellent gift, as the seller suggests. Unwrapping these two pieces of crap would almost be worse than opening a box of *actual* crap, and actual crap is probably less toxic.

32

JACK HAMMER & CHRISTIE PEACH: BAD TASTE BEARS

LOCATION:

Winter Springs, FL

COST:

$19.95 + S/H

DESCRIPTION:

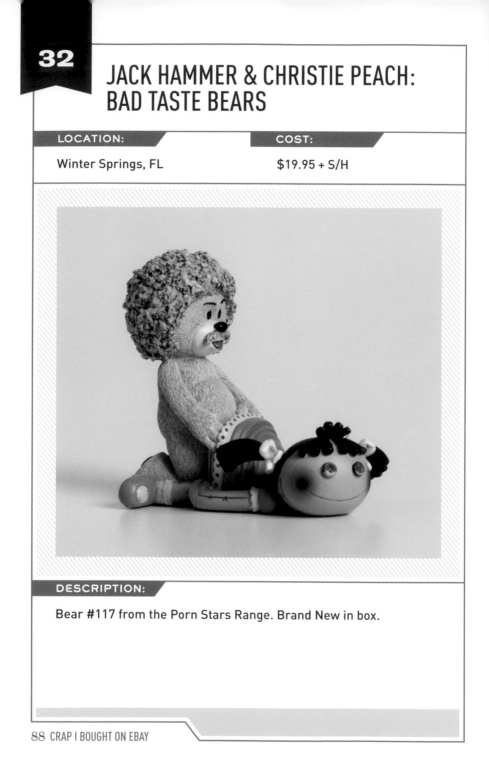

Bear #117 from the Porn Stars Range. Brand New in box.

Hey, we work in offices too, so we understand how hard it is to spice up your cubicle and add a touch of your own personal flair to your corporate trappings. If you're tired of looking at lame bobbleheads and snow globes, perhaps what you need is a small statue of a teddy bear with an Afro and a porn 'stache giving a rag doll a good schtupping. We're pretty sure you'd be the only one in your office to have one!

Even better news: there's a whole line of Bad Taste Bears, so you can express your fondness for everything from hookers to bondage, from slasher films to I.V. drugs! It was tough for us to select just one bear figurine; we had our eye on both the anatomically correct naked bear holding his trench coat open in the classic "flasher" pose, and the little sweetie enjoying the suction of her vacuum cleaner in a somewhat unsanitary manner. Ultimately, we thought that old Jack Hammer here pretty much summed up the Bad Taste Bears.

Judging by the satisfied smile on her face, we think Christie Peach agrees. She may not agree tomorrow when she wakes up from her roofie daze and tries to piece together how she lost her panties and her memory and gained a scathing case of herpes, but that's not our problem.

33

DINOSAUR DUNG FOSSIL

LOCATION:

Nephi, UT

COST:

$5.99 + shipping

DESCRIPTION:

Up for bid is a Fantastic 330 GRAM SLAB of Dinosaur Dung. This dung is a solid chunk and real unique. This is one outstanding specimen with awesome dung pattern .This is 330 GRAMS and is an awesome pile of poop. This chunk is one of the most interesting pieces of SH— you will ever see. It is 6" x 5" x ¼" thick. THIS IS ONE OF A KIND POOP!!!!!!

Since dinosaurs as big as Mack trucks once roamed the Earth before a catastrophic event reduced them all to ash, we guess it just makes sense that they would leave behind a lot of dung. Luckily for us crap-lovers, that dung is now available in all sorts of sizes, shapes, and colors, proving once again that eBay has the perfect pile of poop for everyone!

The fact that you can purchase fossilized dinosaur shit on eBay didn't shock us, but what did shock us was how many *other people* seemed to want to buy it. In fact, it took us no fewer than four tries to get this lovely specimen of a dinosaur's last meal into our greedy little hands.

Interestingly, most of these specimens seem to hail from Utah. We've never been to Utah, but now we'll forever equate that state with dinosaur droppings. Well, dinosaur droppings and polygamy, of course—they might as well put them on the license plate.

↗ Dear Dung Slinger,

Is this really dinosaur dung? This is fake, right? Just looks like a rock to me.

S. Finkter

↗ Dear S. Finkter,

Yes, that's what it is.

Dung Slinger

This guy's a real straight-shooter.

↗ Dear Dung Slinger,

Can you tell what the dinosaur's last meal was? Are there, like, Fred Flintstone bones and shit in there?

S. Finkter

↗ Dear S. Finkter,

Definitely shit, but I can't tell exactly. If you took it to a lab they could probably dissect it and find all kinds of stuff like bits of bone, plant, scales, etc.

Dung Slinger

At least he's honest. Dinosaurs were huge, mean, and if they'd lived alongside humans (which they didn't), they probably would have eaten cavemen like they were jalapeño poppers. They did, however, take a lot of massive dumps in the great state of Utah, so that when they died we could have bidding wars over who gets to purchase their crystallized meadow muffins.

34

PIECE OF HISTORY: CARPET FROM WATERGATE OFFICE

LOCATION:

Milwaukee, WI

COST:

$0.99

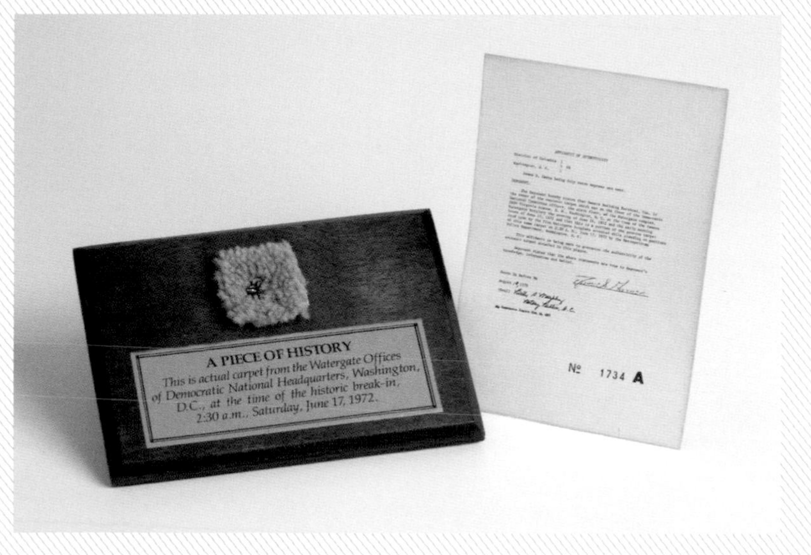

DESCRIPTION:

I suppose people will collect anything, but when I saw this at a rummage sale, I thought it was really kind of weird. This is actual carpet from the Watergate Offices of Democratic National Headquarters, Washington, D.C., at the time of the historic break-in, 2:30 a.m., Saturday, June 17, 1972. It actually comes with a certificate of authenticity that was glued on the back, but this one the glue no longer holds. I did see one other one on eBay, and they must have been sold with different types of bugs on the carpet. This one looks like a green and black spider.

This seller said a mouthful: people will collect anything! We were counting on that fact when we started writing this book.

Now, we can't say for sure whether this one-inch-square section of tan carpet actually came from the Watergate office, but we thought it was funny that someone would want to own a piece of carpet mounted on a plaque, regardless.

Really, the one thing about this item that *isn't* funny is the stupid plastic insect. You know that the dork who owns this thing keeps it in his office and loves when visitors ask about it so that he can say, "Yes, and it's *bugged*, see? Get it? HA HA HA HA!" Nerd.

Frankly, we'd be more likely to believe that this item is the side project of some underpaid carpet salesman than an actual piece of carpet from the office of the Democratic National Committee back in 1972. It just has "big fat fake scam" written all over it, despite the "letter of authenticity" on the back. Besides, we'd like to believe that our government offices may have nicer carpet than this ugly tan shag crap. Maybe something in Berber?

We wondered what would happen if we dared run a black light over these carpet fibers. Would we find DNA flecks glowing like a comforter cover at Red Roof Inn? Would we find evidence of *All the President's Men* sprinkled liberally throughout this tiny thatch of tired tan carpet? Maybe one of Marilyn Monroe's pubic hairs wedged in there? One of those babies would probably fetch quite a price on eBay. After all, people will collect anything.

35

BIZARRE MEXICAN FISH BOBBLEHEAD

LOCATION: Waterloo, IL

COST: $4.49

DESCRIPTION:

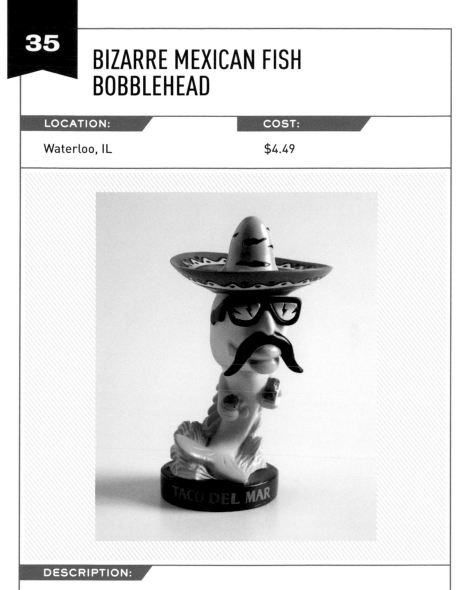

Cool and unusual 6" Taco Del Mar Mexican Fish bobblehead ("Carlos") made of rubberized plastic. Was distributed around 1998-99 and exclusively sold from same name restaurant near Seattle, WA. Quite a conversation piece, how scarce can they be now?

Please say hello to Mr. Carlos Del Mar, former mascot for the fast food chain Taco Del Mar. We say former not because the chain filed for bankruptcy in 2010, but because Carlos tragically took his own life a year prior.

After being discovered in a Tijuana cantina in the mid-nineties dispensing chips and salsa to customers from his oversized sombrero, Del Mar was signed to an exclusive six-figure deal to represent the growing taco chain in America. He quickly rose to superstardom in the world of food chain mascots, overtaking legends like Ronald McDonald, the Arby's hat, and the Quiznos mutant talking rats (or whatever the fuck they are) to become the most popular fast food icon in America.

However, as he would later point out in his autobiography, *Confessions of a Chocho*, Del Mar was never fully comfortable portraying a fish taco because of its crude association with the vagina. He wrote: "Everywhere I go, somebody's talking shit to me, saying stuff like, 'Hey man, wash that thing!' or 'Evening, ladies!' or sniffing the air like they smell me. I laugh it off, but deep down, it really hurts. I'm a fish, not a shark. I have feelings."[1]

Just months after his book was published, Carlos was blamed after several restaurant customers discovered pubic hair in their fish tacos and sued the chain. He was fired as mascot, went into hiding, and was later found dead in his home, charred beyond recognition after throwing himself onto a grill and cooking too long. Carlos' remains were turned over to his former employer. Rumors persist to this day that the chain served him to customers when it began having financial problems.

[1] *Confessions of a Chocho* by Carlos Del Mar, page 84

36

TOILET LIGHTER WITH BLUE TORCH

LOCATION: Connecticut, USA

COST: $0.01

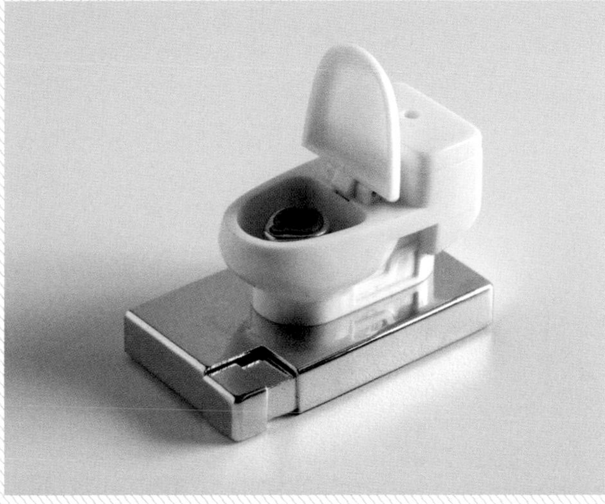

DESCRIPTION:

Refillable lighter with adjustable flame. The Lighter Has a Blue Torch Flame. The actual color of the lighter may vary from the one that is pictured.

Looking for the perfect way to light your farts, pranksters? Look no further! This is one classy lighter. It reminds us of the days when suave folk like Marlene Dietrich and Humphrey Bogart smoked in order to look glamorous. Bogart used one of these toilet lighters, didn't he? We think he must have—after all, he was a charming, sophisticated dude.

That's what we think when we see this toilet-shaped butane lighter: *sophisticated*. There could be no other word to describe a blue flame leaping out of a tiny toilet bowl, after all. Okay, maybe there's one other word: *terrifying*. White-hot flames shooting out of a toilet? Thanks for the nightmares!

↗ Dear Porcelain Gawd,

Have you used this lighter yourself? Do the chicks dig it?

S. Finkter

↗ Dear S. Finkter,

Yeah, I've used it. Not sure about the chicks 'cause I'm married, but I'll bet they think it's funny!

Porcelain Gawd

↗ Dear Porcelain Gawd,

Cool. I am hoping to score some serious tail with this thing. I think it's slick. I'll be the coolest kid in 7th grade!

S. Finkter

↗ Dear S. Finkter,

I'm glad you like it, and good luck with the tail. LOL

Porcelain Gawd

What a guy! He doesn't even care that he's selling a lighter to a child. This thing is like kiddie catnip, and we all know that little kids playing with lighters are *hilarious*. Hope you've got insurance.

CRAP NOBODY NEEDS

BUT SOMEONE WILL BUY IT ANYWAY

It must be nice to have so much money that you can blow it on crap like a helmet to fight zombies, or real estate on the moon, or an inflatable woman who's not meant for sex. The world is lousy with suckers, and it makes us want to create our own crap to sell:

DESCRIPTION: A litter box full of cat turds that recreate the Battle of Little Bighorn. Do my cat's bowels know what really happened? What secrets of this fateful battle can her excrement unlock? Rare and delightful! Bidding starts at $19.95. Hurry before it's gone. (S/H extra.)

37

DONKEY MASK WITH SOUND

LOCATION:

New York, USA

COST:

$10.99

DESCRIPTION:

This auction is for a donkey MASK which actually makes a donkey sound! Awesome! Simply press on the nose & hee-haa! Attached with a convenient headband. Even has simulated teeth . . . so cute!! Suitable for adult or child! IDEAL for school play, manger scene, pretend play & even the SHREK DONKEY!

Hey, jackass! Love your mask! What? It's not a mask? Oops. Sorry. This donkey mask isn't like most donkey masks, and by that we mean ones that actually resemble donkeys. We bought this one because it looks like a lobotomy patient decided to stick big ears and a large tuft of pubic hair on his protective skull cap so he could run around acting like a demented douche nozzle.

What makes this mask truly unique, though, is a button on the nose that, when pushed, makes the most horrendous and annoying sound you've ever heard in your entire life: half bray, half cackle, and all fingernails-on-chalkboard abhorrent.

This button is also a canny defense mechanism for the mask. Should anyone get sick of the wearer's bad behavior—and they will—a punch to the nose will merely set off this ear-shriveling sound again. So the wearer is spared a beating and can continue his boorish mirth at will.

The seller suggests using this mask as part of a nativity scene, and we love that idea. They are solemn events, all quiet and reverential and stuff, which is a total bore. You also never get a coffee break. That makes two good reasons to wear this mask and annoy the shit out of people with your hee-hawing until they get angry and leave.

If that doesn't work, drop your pants and casually squeeze out a big dump right in front of them, then scratch the ground a couple of times and give a good HEEE HAWWW.

That's what a real jackass would do.

38

ZOMBIE DEFENSE HELMET/BRAIN PROTECTOR

LOCATION:	COST:
Christiansburg, VA	$9.99

DESCRIPTION:

This unit has been rated to withstand the teeth of a class 3 zombie (non-magically revived), though we cannot guarantee that it will withstand a class 4 (magic changes a lot of factors). As this unit does not have a face shield, do watch out for face bites. We guarantee that this will be effective in a zombie uprising, though if a class 3 DOES make it through to your brain, we will refund the purchase price minus shipping.

Got an old-school helmet lying around your mom's attic? If so, you're in luck; there's a burgeoning group of consumers out there who want to protect their noggins against vicious zombie attacks. With a little creative marketing, your old motorcycle or football gear can be magically transformed into a Zombie Defense Helmet!

And just like that, you're a geek. Hey, we don't make the rules; that one is dictated by society. Do the math: Zombie Defense Gear + job at GameStop - girlfriend = Geek. Sorry. Just telling you how it is.

Being a geek isn't so bad, though. In fact, this seller makes it seem kind of fun! It helps if you fully commit to the idea that zombies are a real-life threat, even though nothing says "I never get laid" more than living in a fantasy world of zombies, sprites, warlocks, fairies, runes, wizards, gnomes, dragons, elfin magic, and other lame shit that doesn't exist. Of course, we had questions:

↗ Dear ZombieH8r,

This helmet looks kind of beaten up. How many battles has she seen?

S. Finkter

↗ Dear S. Finkter,

This helm has withstood the onslaught of the zombie hordes many a time. Alas, its previous owner forgot to wear his body armor on his last patrol, and the helm returned to us on the opposite side . . . . Thanks for your interest, good luck against the undead hordes!

ZombieH8r

Wow. He really commits. Now we're 100 percent certain that he's never seen a real live naked woman.

39

ALL ABOUT DUNG DVD

LOCATION: Oklahoma City, OK

COST: $2.99

DESCRIPTION:

This video investigates the historical, medical, scientific, and evolutionary importance of poop on an excremental safari guaranteed to fascinate even the most squeamish of viewers. This in-depth look at the history of dung showcases its many other uses. It was a major component in early explosives, is the source of the world's most expensive coffee, can charge a cell phone, and may even help solve some energy and food concerns today. In this epic odyssey, through natural and human history, our aversion to poop just might turn into an understanding of how miraculous and essential the stuff really is.

Pop some popcorn, unplug the phone, and hang a "Do Not Disturb" sign on the door—it's movie night! Let's curl up and watch something truly enlightening and inspiring, something that answers quintessential questions about life on this planet, something that makes us think, laugh, and clap our hands over our mouths to keep ourselves from vomiting. Wait . . . what? Say that last part again?

Oh, should we have mentioned that the movie we're watching is all about bum nuggets? You know: manure, turds, dung, doo doo, poop, excrement, and yes—crap! Call it what you will; this is a documentary about all of the many wonderful crap facts that you never wanted to know about.

Let's be real: is there ever a time when you're going to want to pop this DVD in and learn more about cow plops? If you're determined to watch shit on TV, do what everyone else does and just watch *Jersey Shore*. At least then you won't be left wondering if there's a dookie in your morning joe.

Just remember this awesome DVD description next time you're examining your morning dump before flushing (shut up, we all do it). Don't think of it as repulsive, think of it as "miraculous" and "essential." And then spray some air freshener, would ya? That shit still stinks.

40

TITLE DEEDS FOR MOON PROPERTY

LOCATION:

West Melbourne, FL

COST:

$12.50 (free shipping!)

DESCRIPTION:

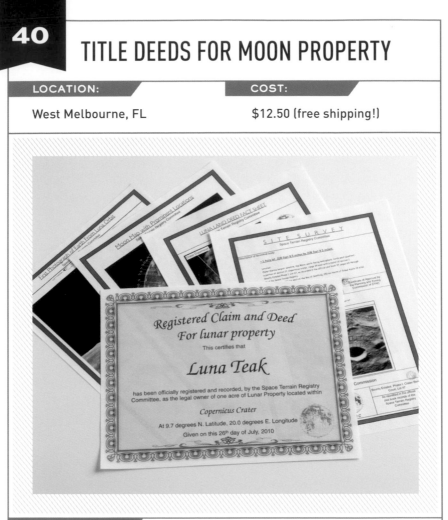

1 ACRE LOTS IN THE PRISTINE SOUTH EAST AREA OF CRATER COPERNICUS KNOWN AS BOUNTY ESTATES. PERSONALIZED CLAIM & DEED CERTIFICATES READY FOR FRAMING. SITE SURVEY OF YOUR LAND.

For a mere twelve dollars and fifty cents, you can own a full acre of land on a desolate hunk of rock with sub-zero temperatures and none of the pesky annoyances of gravity or oxygen. Sure, humans haven't set foot on the moon since 1969, but that doesn't mean there isn't a booming real estate market up there.

In fact, this seller claims there is an entire housing development in the works on the moon called Bounty Estates, and over 2.7 million Earthlings, including astronauts Buzz Aldrin and Neil Armstrong, have already staked their claim on some prime lunar real estate. And those guys know from moon lots, do they not? Still, we needed more info before making such an important purchase, so we contacted the seller.

↗ Dear Spaceball,

I have a small alpaca farm and am wondering if Bounty Estates is zoned for farms?

S. Finkter

Lord knows we've had enough trouble with our neighbors here on Earth because of these so-called zoning laws they're always going on and on about. Best to go ahead and settle this now before purchasing a moon lot and moving all our livestock up there, only to be turned away.

↗ Dear S. Finkter,

No problem at all. You can set anything you want on your land.

Spaceball

Well, that's certainly a relief. Another question:

↗ Dear Spaceball,

Thank you so much! Now, in your listing you mentioned that famous astronauts have also purchased lots in Bounty Estates. Any chance I could be neighbors with Buzz Aldrin? I'm a big fan. His wife seems nice, too. I think we'd get along great! If not, that's okay, but can you tell me anything about the other residents? I want to know who my neighbors would be.

S. Finkter

We saw Buzz on *Dancing with the Stars* and he seems like a great dude. We can just picture kicking back on our porches, watching the alpacas graze in their custom-made spacesuits, and drinking some ice-cold Tang through our breathing apparatuses.

↗ Dear S. Finkter,

Sure, just tell me who you want your neighbors to be, buy a lot, and I'll make it happen.

Spaceball

Score! Is this seller accommodating or what? We can choose *anyone we want* to be our neighbors and he'll make it happen. The guy is positively magical! However, since this seller also sells land on Mars, Venus, Pluto, and "The Solar System," we probably should do a little more research before committing to living on the moon. Alpacas might prefer the climate on Uranus.

ALCOHOLICS ANONYMOUS (AA) 12-STEP CARD GAME

LOCATION:

Niceville, FL

COST:

$6.99

DESCRIPTION:

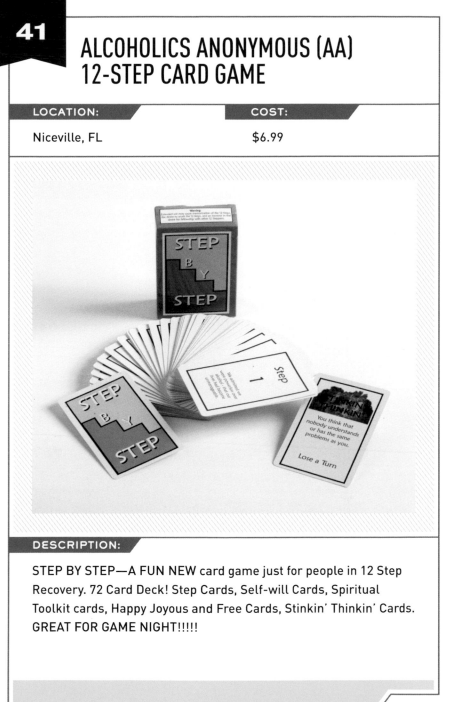

STEP BY STEP—A FUN NEW card game just for people in 12 Step Recovery. 72 Card Deck! Step Cards, Self-will Cards, Spiritual Toolkit cards, Happy Joyous and Free Cards, Stinkin' Thinkin' Cards. GREAT FOR GAME NIGHT!!!!!

We've got nothing against drunks—some of our best friends and most of our immediate family are hopeless alcoholics—but we don't think a FUN NEW game is really what they need.

They've had enough fun—that's how they ended up in a twelve-step program in the first place. They might not remember it, but they did—we've got the pictures and bail receipts to prove it. Now fun time's over. They need work, not homemade card games. Penance. Suffering. Meetings. Lots and lots of meetings.

In AA, they tell recovering alcoholics that when they stop drinking, they will find themselves with a surprising amount of free time. That's how we suspect this game came to be. Some sop with nothing better to do got hopped up on Camels and bad coffee and decided to cook up a FUN NEW card game for his new AA buddies. Unfortunately, the game looks like a real bore, and you know what a bored drunk will do: drink.

The object of the game is to collect all twelve-step cards quicker than your opponents. Just like in real life, though, your journey to sobriety has obstacles in the form of Stinkin' Thinkin' and Self-will cards, which dock you a turn for bad behaviors. This is where we see some missed opportunities to jazz up the game.

Instead of punishing the player for things like feeling sorry for himself or forgetting to call his sponsor (yawn), we'd like to see Self-will and Stinkin' Thinkin' cards with more authenticity and higher stakes. For example:

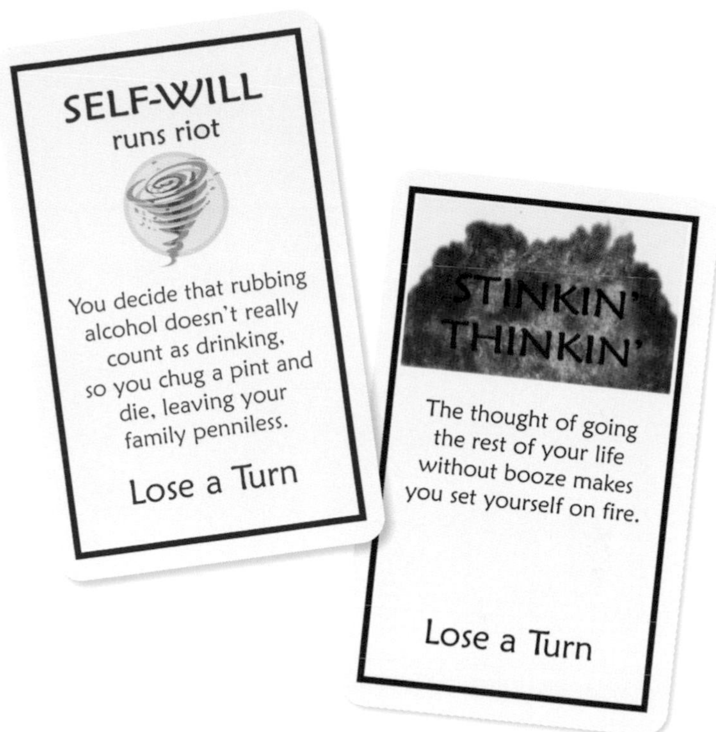

SELF-WILL
runs riot
You decide that rubbing
alcohol doesn't really
count as drinking,
so you chug a pint and
die, leaving your
family penniless.
Lose a Turn
STINKIN'
THINKIN'
The thought of going
the rest of your life
without booze makes
you set yourself on fire.
Lose a Turn

Now that's a game we might play. We might even turn it into a drinking game.

42

RARE SPELL: HAVE AND CONTROL YOUR OWN CLONE

LOCATION:	COST:
Belchertown, MA	$5.99

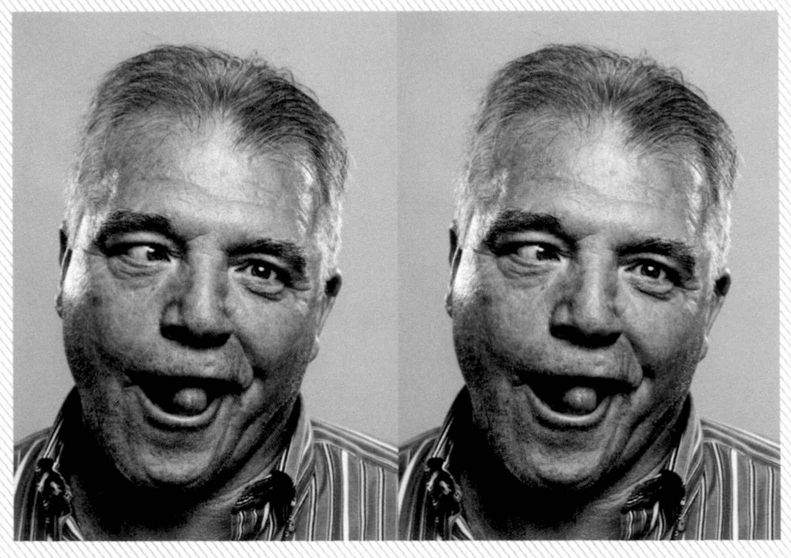

DESCRIPTION:

Have you ever wondered what it would be like to have an exact clone of yourself? A person who looked and acted just like you? This spell can do that. Imagine the possibilities. You could have the clone go into work for you while you relax on the beach. You have complete control over your personal clone. It will obey your every command. It has every skill and ability that you have. Be in two places at once, complete unpleasant tasks, get more done, get two jobs at once, or even find more lovers.

We have a confession to make. We didn't even write this book; we each bought ourselves a clone and went on vacation while our clones slaved away at their computers for weeks at a time. That's why there are so many typos; clones suck at proofreading.

Nah, we're joking, and when we saw this listing we thought the seller must be joking, too. However, a quick conversation with her proved that she was serious when she claimed to be a witch who could conjure identical clones for a very modest sum. It was a hard concept to wrap our minds around, but it *would* explain a lot. For instance, maybe this is why Kenny Rogers hasn't looked like himself in many years, or why Cher never ages. The idea of having our own clones grew on us, though. We started to think about possible uses.

↗ Dear Crazy Witch Lady,

Is the clone flesh and blood? Will it know all of my secrets? Can I use it to rob a bank? Thanks.

S. Finkter

Not that we'd ever do *that*. **shifty-eyed**

↗ Dear S. Finkter,

Once the clone forms, it is flesh and blood. It will behave how you behave with one exception: it will obey all of your commands. It will do whatever you want it to.

It will have all of the skills and knowledge that you have. So, it will know all of your secrets. I don't recommend using it to do illegal things. This could get the authorities after you because you look exactly the same as the clone. I can't endorse that sort of activity.

For maximum results, I recommend a triple or quadruple cast. These are the strongest spells that I have and will help you to see the most effective results.

Crazy Witch Lady

Well, duh! Why didn't we think of that? We wonder if "It wasn't me, it was a clone of me that I bought on eBay" is a valid excuse in a court of law. Probably not.

↗ Dear Crazy Witch Lady,

If I have sex with my clone, is that technically cheating? People are always telling me to go fuck myself, and I'd like to give it a try.

S. Finkter

tap tap tap Hello? Is this thing on?

43

LIFE-SIZED INFLATABLE WOMAN

LOCATION:

Salt Lake City, UT

COST:

$13.00 + S/H

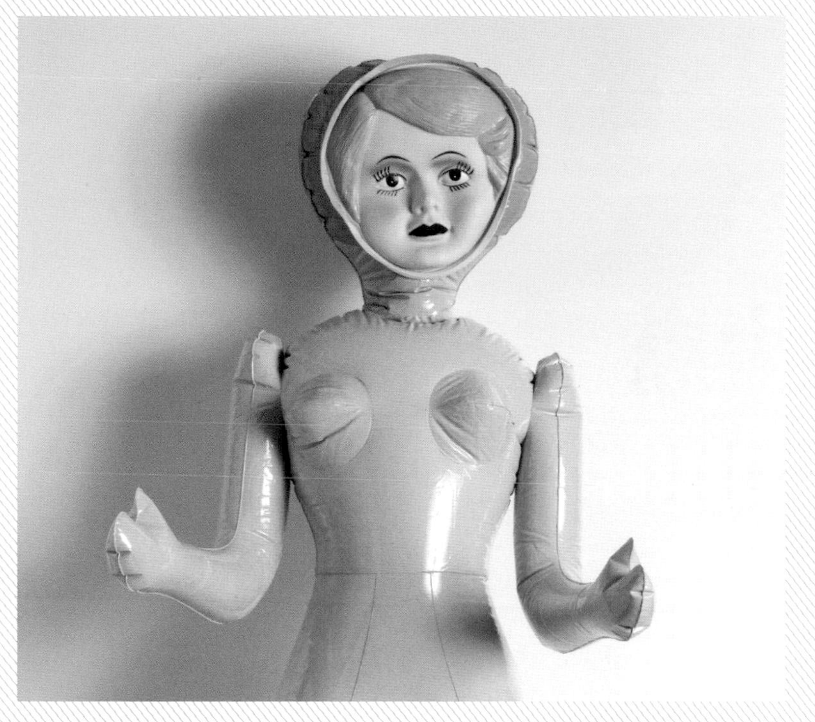

DESCRIPTION:

This gal is 5 foot tall! Fun way to display your clothes & accessories. Works great for store displays. Boost your sales by showing what you've got. Put her in your store window. Pose her as you like. She's your flexible mannequin. You can also have a lot of fun with her. Put her in the pool. Use express lane with her. Easy to inflate. Easy to store.

Just so we're clear: this is not a sex doll. You'll find no input holes anywhere on her; she's just not that kind of girl. According to the listing, she's a *model* and would look great in a toy store flaunting your wares.

At first we were skeptical about her modeling skills, since, let's face it: when was the last time you saw a five-foot-tall model with legs that end in stumps? Yet you'll notice our gal came in quite handy at the *Crap I Bought on eBay* photo shoot—Vicky Vinyl here turned out to be quite the star of our raunchy and ridiculous fashion show. Unlike real models, she didn't even complain when we gave her an enormous bush or made her wear a pair of elephant trunk *man*ties. She was a real pro.

Since she was useful as our model, we can go ahead and ignore the fact that she looks like some sort of Amish love doll. We wondered if anyone ever bought one of these dolls accidentally while trying to purchase a cheap sex doll. What a disappointment that would be; you get her inflated to find you can't fuck her, you can't manipulate her into any good positions, and you can only have one-sided conversations with her. If she also criticized your driving, she'd be exactly like your ex-wife.

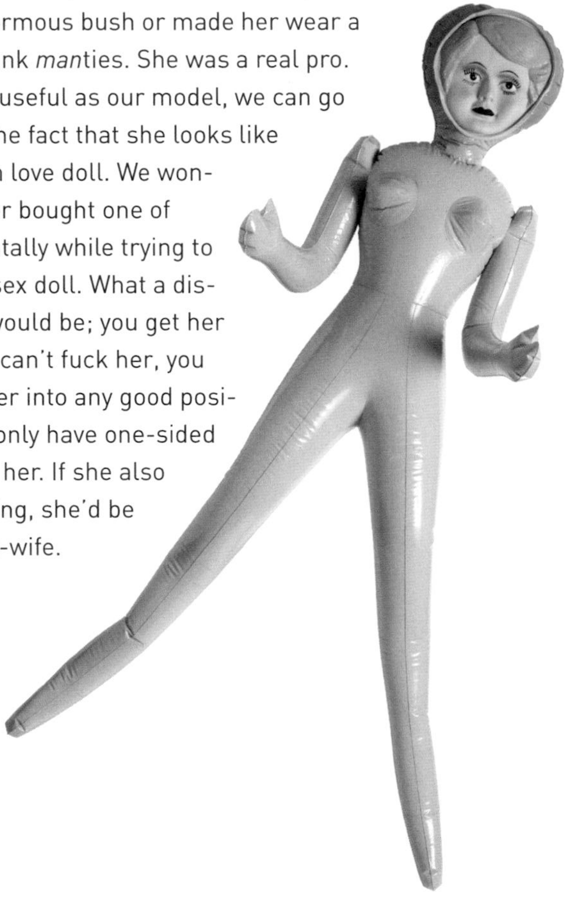

CRAP FOR YOUR JUNK

YOUR BUSINESS IS YOUR BUSINESS

For anyone reading this book who has ever had a cold scrotum, this chapter is for you. For those with bald crotches and flat nipples, this chapter is for you. If you have a hairy ass and back, a foreskin that was removed against your will, or a butt plug that doesn't have disco lights in it, this chapter is for you. This chapter is a labor of love from us to all of you whose genitals have never known the joy and comfort that a visit to eBay can bring. We do this because we love you, and we care about your junk.

44

GREEN CAMO TRAP DOOR WILLIE WARMER

LOCATION: Phoenix, AZ

COST: $12.99

DESCRIPTION:

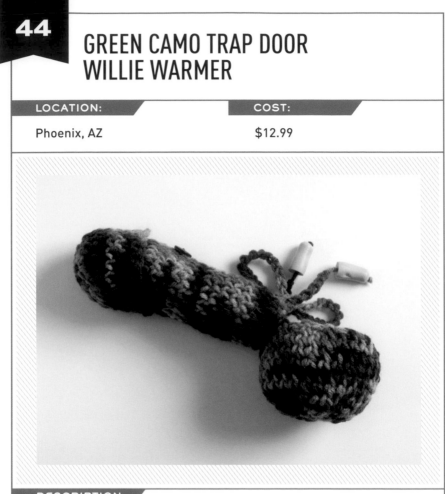

Made from comfortable yarns is a new and hand crocheted original. A fun way to bring a smile to your hunter or serviceman. Ample room and easily cinched up with a comfort draw string that snuggles all the parts together. Trap door has button closing, which can make it a one piece sock and the total length of shaft is 6 inches, but with the trap door unbuttoned and down means one size fits all! Hand washable and air dry.

Guys: ever found yourself sitting high up in a tree in early February, waiting for a deer to come along so you can blow a gaping hole in its ass with a high-powered rifle, and said to yourself, "Forsooth, 'tis a frigid morrow that vexeth me. My manhood acheth as if bound in spring floe"?

Neither have we, but someone must, because eBay is filthy with these hand-crocheted penis socks designed to keep a man's junk toasty no matter what the temperature. We chose this one because it's camouflaged and, hey, if you ever get the urge to hunt without pants—some people do—you don't want the glare of your pasty white sun-starved schlong alerting the quarry to your presence.

Never mind that you'll be scratching your itchy, yarn-covered wiener so hard, every animal within a fifteen-mile radius will hear you and flee.

Clearly, much time and thought went into the innovative design and loving craftsmanship of this thing, from the drawstring for snugness (ouch) to the handy front opening for the call of nature—or a sudden urge to masturbate in the middle of the woods.

Our favorite part, though, is the testicle cup. Balls generally stay warm, even in cold weather, so we may wear the Willy Warmer backward and give our penis a little Rastafarian hat, as demonstrated below on Mr. T.

Jah and I pity dee fool, mon.

45

MERKIN PUBIC WIG

LOCATION: Hollywood, FL

COST: $36.95

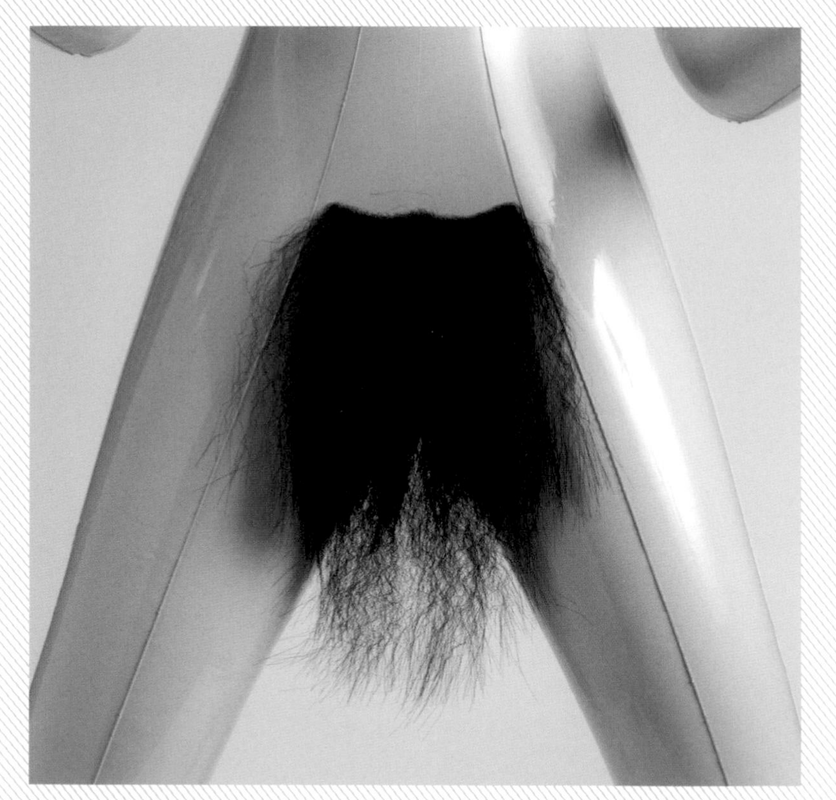

DESCRIPTION:

MERKIN ONLY IN BLACK. USED DURING MIDDLE AGES OR TODAY FOR WOMEN. VERY WELL MADE FROM A LEADING WIG MANUFACTURER. ALL SALES FINAL. FLORIDA LAW DOES NOT ALLOW RETURNS ON WIGS.

If you're as tired of looking at bald vulvas as we are, you'll be relieved to know that you can still purchase a quality faux muff from the comfort of your home. Next time you get a little overzealous with the wax or razor, simply slip on this little black number and let your inner flower child strut her stuff! The listing doesn't explain what a merkin is, though, so we decided to feign ignorance and have a little fun with the seller.

↗ Dear PubeHocker,

Nice goatee. It's a goatee, right? How do I get it to stay on?

S. Finkter

↗ Dear S. Finkter,

No, a merkin is used to cover a woman's private part, or it can be used as chest hair.

PubeHocker

Chest hair? This guy's chest hair might look like pubes, but ours doesn't.

↗ Dear PubeHocker,

Thanks. Is it made from real pubes? I'm really hairy and I have tons of pubes I could sell or donate. Do you know how I could make that happen?

S. Finkter

It has been four days. He probably won't answer, but we've been saving our pube trimmings *just in case*. If he doesn't want them, there's always Locks of Love.

46

DISCO LIGHT-UP VIBRATING BUTT PLUG

LOCATION: Farmington, NM

COST: $9.95

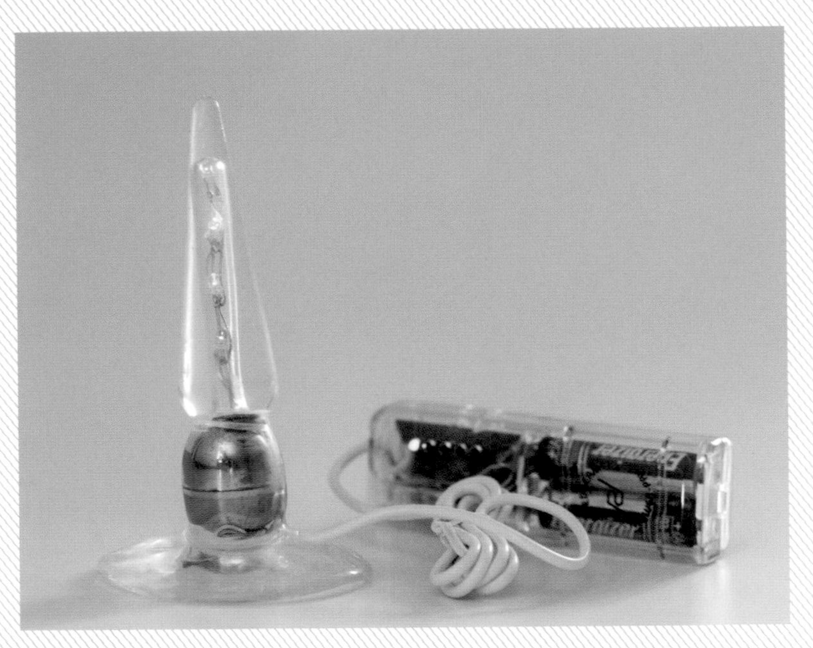

DESCRIPTION:

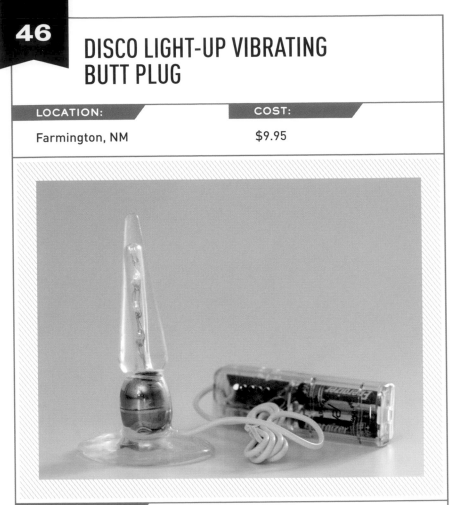

This soft silicone butt plug vibrates wildly as the exciting disco lights show the way to pure satisfaction. Completely adjustable vibration speed is set on the corded, LED slide control unit. 2 AA batteries, not included 4 inches long 1 inches wide 3 inches around. Private Listing—anyone can buy butt no one can tell what was purchased. Very Discreet!

Finally—a toy that tells the world, "There's a party in my ass! Everybody's coming!"

If you aren't up to speed on your sexual deviance, a butt plug is an object that you shove up your anus for sexual gratification. It is not, as the name might imply, intended to plug the ass to prevent things from coming out—although if you've ever had diarrhea, you'd kill for something like that.

Butt plugs have other uses as well, but we'll let you investigate those on your own since the mere idea of the thing makes us clench our buttcheeks tighter than the vault at Fort Knox.

A plug typically has one end that's wide to keep it from slipping into your rectum and getting stuck, making it a preferable alternative to things like dildos, broomsticks, baseballs, rodents, soda bottles, paint rollers, fruit, vegetables, action figures, umbrellas, batons, and other stuff that will land you in the ER and require you to explain to a doctor why you have a lava lamp up your ass. Not fun.

In this case, the wide end has disco lights that put on a show, which sounds mildly amusing but mostly pointless to us. If you're so horny that you want to stick a large hunk of vibrating plastic up your butt, disco dancing is probably the last thing on your mind.

Clearly the Disco Light-Up Vibrating Butt Plug is made for the white elephant office gift exchange crowd, as it is the kind of item guaranteed to get you lots of laughs—and a pink slip. Or a pink sock.

47

SILICONE NIPPLE ENHANCERS

LOCATION: San Gabriel, CA

COST: $8.48

DESCRIPTION:

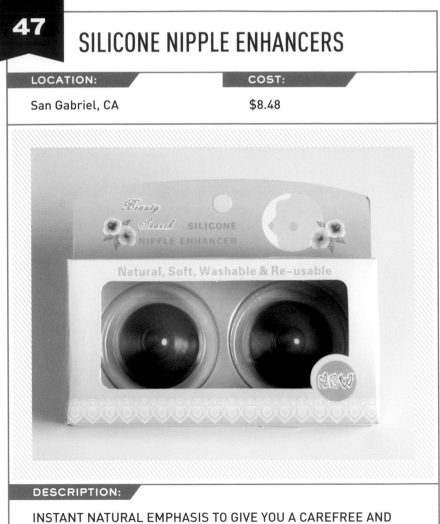

INSTANT NATURAL EMPHASIS TO GIVE YOU A CAREFREE AND SEXY LOOK. FUN "ALL-EYES-ON-ME LOOK" AND COMFORTABLE FOR ALL DAY WEAR. CAN BE WORN WITH BRAS, SWIMMING SUITS, DRESSES, GOWNS, LINGERIE, AND T-SHIRTS FOR IMMEDIATE NIPPLE ENHANCEMENT. Colors: Pink or Mocha

Is it cold in here or is it just our giant fake nipples? Most women spend a lot of time making sure that the headlights *aren't* showing, but there are a few exhibitionists among us who want to make sure that all eyes are on the money-makers. Yes, we're talking about strippers.

We have heard that strippers love these fake nips. Not that we'd know. **cough** We have a friend who once asked a stripper whether her perky nipples were real or not. She replied that they were *not* real, but didn't elaborate lest she spoil her mystique. Now that we've found these silicone turbo-pokies on eBay, we think we've got her secret all figured out.

One thing is clear: Wearing these bad boys will get you noticed by horny sweater-gazers faster than you can say, "Turkey's done!"

↗ Dear Gumball Smuggler,

Love these nips! Do they come in 3X? These are a little small for me.

Thanks,

S. Finkter

↗ Dear S. Finkter,

I only have the one size, sorry. They are fairly big. I don't think you will be disappointed.

Gumball Smuggler

↗ Dear Gumball Smuggler,

Perhaps, but my nipples are about twice this size. When I get cold, they stick out like extra digits. I'm talking real glass cutters. Let's put it this way: when I go to the ATM in the winter, I don't have to take my gloves off to use the keypad, if you know what I mean ;)

S. Finkter

↗ Dear S. Finkter,

I'm sorry, but I only have the one size.

Gumball Smuggler

↗ Dear Gumball Smuggler,

Okay. You might consider making bigger ones for gals like me with huge nips. You could use thimbles as a mold.

S. Finkter

No reply.

↗ Dear Gumball Smuggler,

On second thought, thimbles may not be big enough. My nipples look more like baby carrots when they're hard. Maybe an empty Chapstick tube would work better for a mold.

S. Finkter

No reply.

↗ Dear Gumball Smuggler,

Or maybe a glass tube like they use in bars for shots. Thoughts?

S. Finkter

Finally, a reply.

↗ Dear S. Finkter,

Stop contacting me or I will report you to eBay.

Gumball Smuggler

48

UNCIRCUMCISING CONE

LOCATION:

Chicago, IL

COST:

$9

DESCRIPTION:

The Your-Skin® RESTORATION CONE by TLC Tugger® Enjoy sex more through foreskin restoration. Penis Pills? What a joke! Here's honest improvement! If you're circumcised, you have no idea what you're missing. The foreskin was meant to protect your glans from the drying effects of clothing and air, keeping it supple and sensitive. Now you can get back some of the sensation that was taken from you by gently applying tension to the penile shaft skin, which induces it to grow (just like the earlobes on those exotic tribesmen on Discovery Channel). The cone allows you to pull your own skin forward over your glans and keep it there. Nothing allows your glans and "inner" skin to regain health better than a protective sheath of your own skin.

Whoa. Someone's a little bitter about having his schlong trimmed as an infant, huh? Sorry, buddy—the doctor asked what you wanted but you didn't answer, so he went with standard procedure and took that ugly old turtleneck right off. Bet you'll speak up next time, won't you?

Not to be deterred, Bitter Circumcised Guy has a solution: wear this little lampshade on your dick so it looks like it had a little too much to drink at the penis party. You don't even have to take it off to pee. Just use the handy hole in the tip that turns your urine flow into a concentrated laserlike blast with pinpoint accuracy, so you can hit the toilet from across the room without leaving your easy chair. Talk about convenience!

Then one magical day you wake up and voilà: you've grown back your foreskin and your pork sword has regained its original appearance of a napping anteater—one with a huge funnel-shaped goiter growing off its head because your skin has grown around the cone, permanently fusing it with your penis. Oops!

At that point, regaining sensitivity will take a back seat to other concerns, like prying this piece of rubber off your wang without bleeding to death. Suddenly, being circumcised doesn't seem so bad, does it?

Who invited that dickhead to the party?

49

RAZORBA BACK HAIR SHAVER

LOCATION:	COST:
Everywhere! US	$19.95

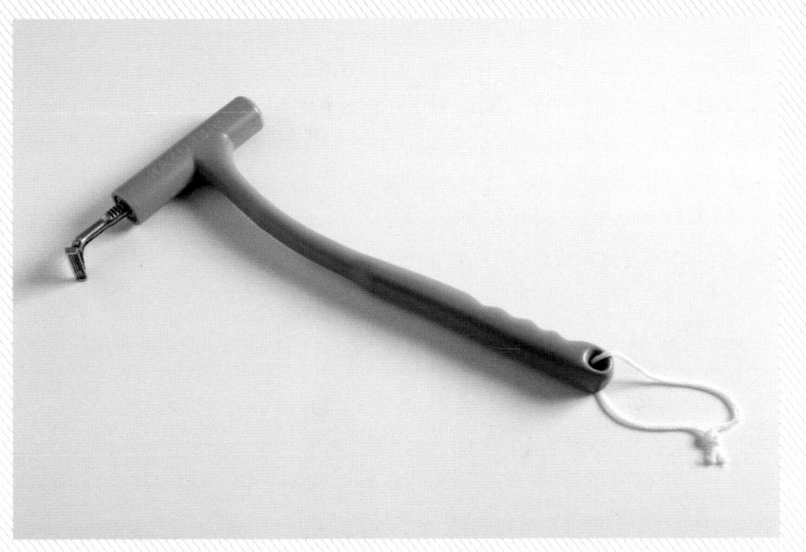

DESCRIPTION:

Back hair is ugly and embarrassing. The Razorba™ ("ray-zor-buh") allows you to shave your back hair painlessly, quickly, easily. And most importantly you do it yourself. No more begging for help. No more embarrassing trips to the salon, or embarrassment at the beach, pool, or basketball court. Salons do NOT want you to buy this product, they make thousands of dollars from men who require regular back waxing. Don't waste money for a back wax that lasts only a few days when you can solve your back hair problem for only $19.95.

Finally, a cure for all that annoying back hair. Why didn't we think of attaching a razor to a stick? **forehead SMACK!**

Wearing a sweater that you can't take off would suck. Some guys, like the Speedo-wearing Italians and Greeks who make pool filters shudder, are proud of their hirsuteness and consider it a sign that they are macho, which is also why they think it's okay to wear a Speedo. It's the other dudes—the bashful guys who wear a t-shirt in the pool—whom we pity. They're the ones so desperate to remove back hair that they would actually buy something like this.

Our seller tells us that salons don't want you to buy this product. Maybe not, but your doctor does. After you shred your back to ribbons and can't stop the bleeding, he'll give you some salve and bandages and then bill your insurance company $850. SCORE! No wonder five out of five physicians recommend Razorba for their own fiscal health.

We had one question for the seller about Razorba.

↗ Dear Sweeney Todd,

God bless you! You are a gift from heaven to those of us with debilitating back fur. Thank you for selling this important product. Question: the Razorba does not appear to be long enough to reach my ass, which is the hairiest part of my body. Is there an attachment available for purchase?

Thanks,

S. Finkter

His reply? A curt "No." That's okay, jag-off, we can cut up a broomstick and make our own extension.

Here's our advice: if you want to shave your back that badly, find a blind guy or someone with a chronic tremor and give them five dollars to do it with a normal razor. The result will be the same, but you'll save fifteen dollars.

PAGING DR. CRAP

AND YOU THOUGHT YOUR MEDICAL PLAN SUCKED

Healthcare is a big deal these days, and as always, we're here to help. Need a new set of chompers or a round of shock treatment or a charcoal muffler for your chronic flatulence? No problem! Since when does a person have to be board-certified to help out a fellow human being? With a little help from eBay, anyone can be a health-care provider, but without all those pesky medical school bills. Even at your worst, you'll still be better than most HMO doctors.

50

100 ACRYLIC DENTURES/FALSE TEETH

LOCATION: St. Petersburg, FL

COST: $10.50

DESCRIPTION:

FOR AUCTION—NEW—100 ACRYLIC DENTURE TEETH/FALSE TEETH. MIXED SHADES AND MOULDS. IDEAL FOR REPAIRS. WILL SHIP WORLDWIDE!

Nobody likes going to the dentist, including us. But we like having teeth that don't prevent us from getting laid, so we jumped at the chance to snag these 100 (count 'em!) fake chompers at such a great price. Do you know what dentists charge for crowns these days?

"Mixed shades and moulds [sic]" means that whichever tooth ails us, we'll have a replacement somewhere in this bunch. Hopefully we'll never need all one hundred of these, and can give some to friends or hand them out to trick-or-treaters on Halloween. In low light they could easily pass for candy corn.

So we got the teeth. Now all we need is some instruction on how to put them in. We figured the seller would know.

↗ Dear Tooferson,

What kind of glue do you recommend using to install these? Or do they come with glue? If not, I have Gorilla Glue, household cement, and Krazy Glue. I'm thinking Gorilla is the way to go.

S. Finkter

Bad news.

↗ Dear S. Finkter,

I cannot advise you on how to install the teeth, only a licensed dentist can do that. This is a sale for the teeth only, no glue included. The teeth are used by licensed dentists and dental technicians.

Tooferson

Oh, come on. Don't BS a BSer.

↗ Dear Tooferson,

Thanks. I understand that you have to say that for legal reasons, but, just between us, can't I do it? I'm pretty good with glue.

S. Finkter

Victory! And look how nice the guy is.

↗ Dear S. Finkter,

As you understand I cannot give you advise [sic], all I can say is you can try and see for yourself! On eBay under denture repair, is a kit for $2.95 you can buy and use to glue the teeth you purchase from me.

Tooferson

So, the story has a happy ending, except for one thing. We accidentally glued our tongue to the roof of our mouth.

Brother, can you spare some teefs?

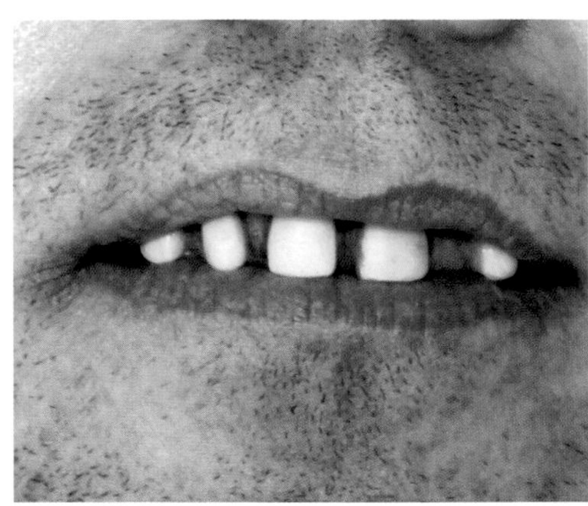

51

FLAT-D FLATULENCE FILTER PAD ODOR/FART CONTROL

LOCATION:

Cedar Rapids, IA

COST:

$12.95

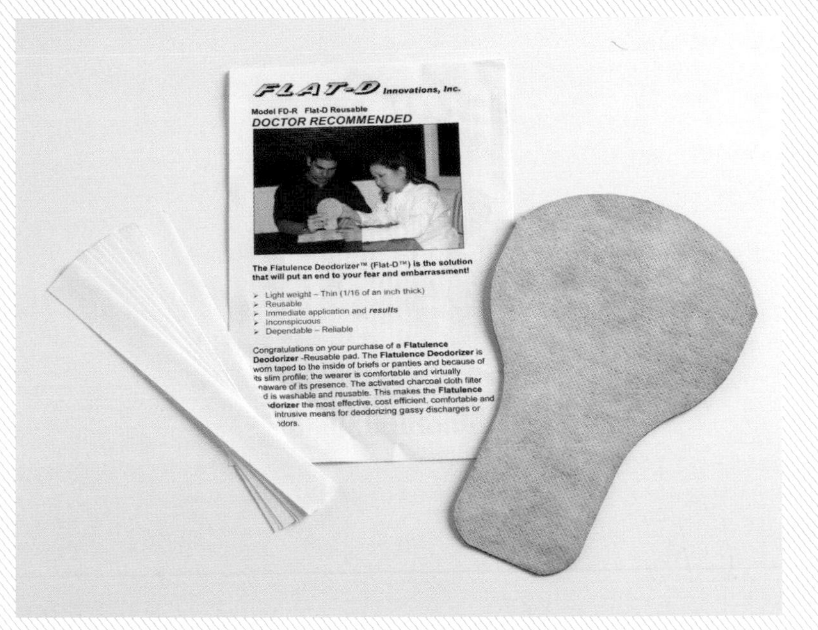

DESCRIPTION:

ODOR CONTROL FOR PENNIES A DAY! Enjoy being around others without the worry! Thousands of these have sold throughout the world. This product is tried and tested. Washable and reusable. Several weeks of use out of each pad. NO STRINGS! NO WORRIES! NO SMELLS! RESOLVE YOUR CONDITION SAFELY AND WITH CONFIDENCE!

We don't know much about Iowa, but where we live, there's an easy way to keep people from smelling your farts. It's called not farting around other people. You know, holding it in until you can get to a restroom or cow pasture or Red Lobster, where you can rip 'em to your heart's content.

Or you can do like our friend Tony and cut one in your jerk of a boss's office every time he steps away from his desk, then snicker to yourself when he bitches about the inexplicable lingering stench of rotten eggs.

Maybe they're big on individual expression in Iowa and encourage people to poot as they please—whenever, wherever, and whoever is around. For freewheeling Iowans and anyone else who can't be bothered to stifle his sphincter, there's Flat-D, the fart filter that promises you *odor control for pennies a day*, an idea anyone can get behind. Heh heh. *Behind*, get it?

The concept is simple, yet revolutionary: just adhere the Flat-D pad to your underdrawers with the included adhesive strips (which doesn't sound uncomfortable at all), and center the business end over your cornhole. Then off you go, secure in the knowledge that you can cut the cheese all day long and no one will smell it. They'll *hear* it, of course—Flat-D isn't a sound filter—but you can always blame it on the dog.

Our only concern with the Flat-D Flatulence Filter is that it is made with activated charcoal powder, which seems like a fire hazard. We also wonder if a cloud of black smoke billows out of your pants every time you let one rip. These are small concerns, though, for such a useful and necessary product.

No strings. No worries. No smells. No shit.

Don't open until Christmas!

52

EM-ESSIST—HANDS-FREE CONTAINMENT OF EMESIS

LOCATION: Anaheim, CA

COST: $7.95

DESCRIPTION:

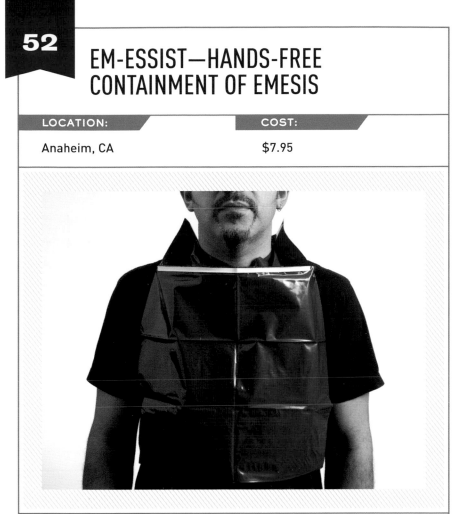

Effective Vomit Management—Motion/Air Sickness Bag. Paramedic-invented product designed with the field provider in mind. Allows "hands-free" containment of emesis (vomit) if patient is unconscious or altered. Wire hoops in neck bib maintains bib position. Wire hoop at entrance of containment bag ensures open and close proximity to patient's mouth, whether patient can hold bag or not. Excellent disposal tool. Dispenser Box of 10.

No, this is not a feed bag, but an innovative tool for effective vomit management. And, if anything is important in this life, it's managing your upchuck. People tend to get upset when they see or smell that stuff; get it on them and they will bitch-slap you. Note that the Em-Essist (clever misspelling intentional) was invented by a paramedic, one who was no doubt tired of wearing other people's regurgitated lunch on his uniform.

Em-Essist, we're told, provides "hands-free containment of emesis (vomit) if patient is unconscious or *altered*," which is a nice way of saying shit-faced and handcuffed in the back seat of a cop car after exposing her tits at the Justin Bieber concert. Believe us when we say that horking in a police car is a good way to get your skull cracked.

If you're a double amputee or simply don't anticipate horking anytime soon, you could always use it as a feed bag. Just fill it up with popcorn or chicken wings or soup (straw required) for a liberating hands-free dining experience at the game, the race, the movie, anywhere.

We're already planning to use ours on Halloween—no bag to carry around, just lean over and let them toss the candy right into the Em-Essist—easy peasy—while your hands stay toasty in your pockets on a cold October night.

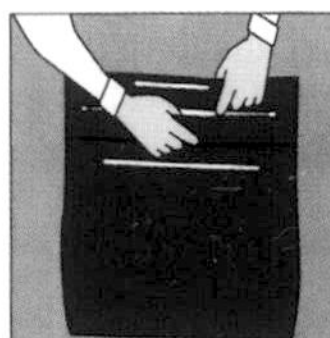

Form hole by opening at top perforation.

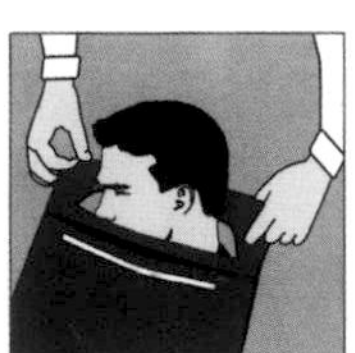

Place patient's head through opening.

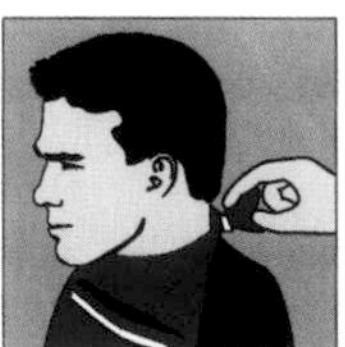

Twist top wire to bring Em-Essist™ close to patient's face.

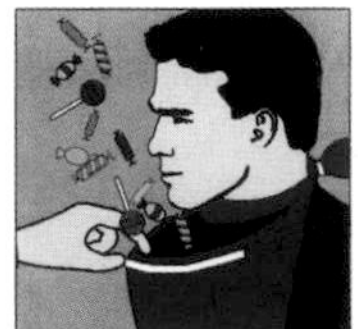

Receive candy.

New products coming soon!

* Ur-Assist for incontinence
* Ass-Ist for sufferers of irritable bowel syndrome

53

VALTREX NOTE PAD

LOCATION:

Ft. Wayne, IN

COST:

$3

DESCRIPTION:

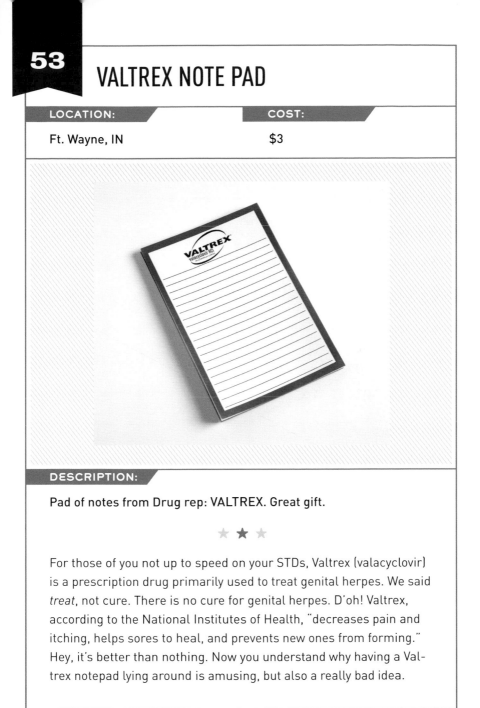

Pad of notes from Drug rep: VALTREX. Great gift.

For those of you not up to speed on your STDs, Valtrex (valacyclovir) is a prescription drug primarily used to treat genital herpes. We said *treat*, not cure. There is no cure for genital herpes. D'oh! Valtrex, according to the National Institutes of Health, "decreases pain and itching, helps sores to heal, and prevents new ones from forming." Hey, it's better than nothing. Now you understand why having a Valtrex notepad lying around is amusing, but also a really bad idea.

VALTREX
valacyclovir HCl
Hi Bill -
Was great meeting you yesterday! :)
Give me a call some time. Maybe we can hang out.
Marci
(555) 299-5356
VALTREX
valacyclovir HCl
Hey Bill -
I'm having a few friends over to watch the game Saturday night. Would love it if you joined us!
No need to bring anything - we'll have plenty of snacks and beer.
Call me!
VALTREX
valacyclovir HCl
Hi Bill -
You missed a fun game!
I'm seeing a client near your office on Thursday. Any chance we could do lunch?
Call me (please :)
Marci
VALTREX
valacyclovir HCl
Bill -
I'm not usually this forward but I really wish you would call me.
You're a great guy and I felt a connection when we met. Was hoping you did, too (?).
Call me, mister!
VALTREX
valacyclovir HCl
Okay, Bill -
Not sure why you won't call me. Have I offended you in some way?
I'm attractive, successful, and nice. I'm also incredible in bed (or so I've been told).
You can judge for yourself if you call me. ;)
Marci
(555) 299-5356
VALTREX
valacyclovir HCl
Bill -
You know what? Don't call me. EVER.
I've been nothing but nice to you, but I guess you're too busy to make a phone call, huh?
FUCK YOU, ASSHOLE!
You have no idea what you're missing.
Marci

54

EXTRA LARGE CHOPPERS/ EDUCATIONAL TEETH

LOCATION:

Lakeland, FL

COST:

$45

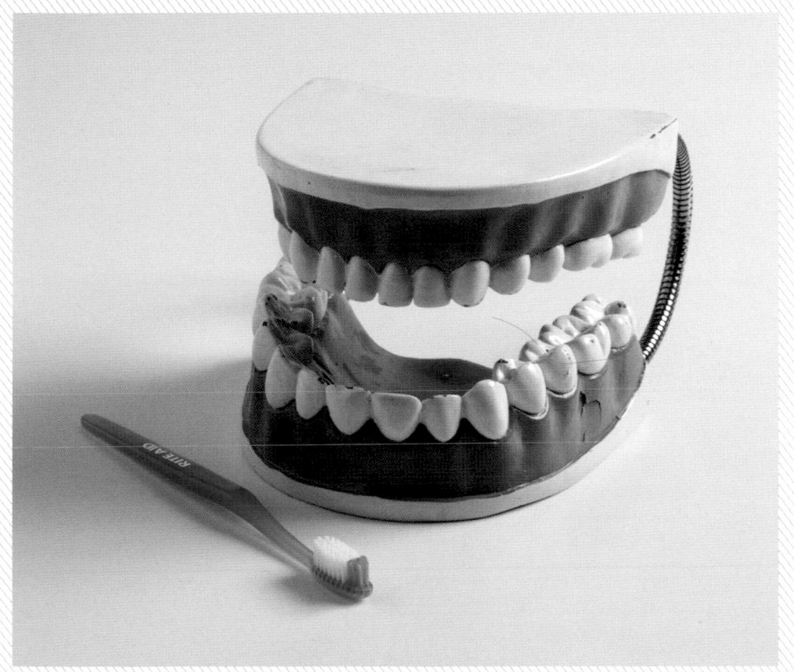

DESCRIPTION:

Extra large teeth for educational demonstration. Perfect for a dentist's office or a science teacher. You can teach the names of the individual teeth, uppers, lowers, eye teeth, molars, etc. The metal bands are bendable like a jaw. You can close the teeth. They will stay closed. Or you can open it all the way and make it flat.

Check it out, we bought Gary Busey's teeth on eBay. How cool is that? He probably hocked them to buy drugs during lean spells between straight-to-TBS movie roles. But we just read in *Variety* that he got cast as Unhinged Assassin #2 in *Under Siege 4: Un-Siege-able*, so he'll be coming into some coin soon and will probably want his chompers back. That's why we just sent him this note:

Dear Gar,

You might not remember but we met you back in 1998 in Toronto. You were staying in the room next to us at the Four Seasons, and, well, if you will excuse our candor, you were a total dick. We're talking, like, Mel Gibson levels of ass-wipe, but without the credentials to justify it.

But hey, we're sorry the sound of our breathing disturbed your beauty sleep. If we'd known you were shooting an important picture like *Another Hider in the House*, we would've kept it down.

Anyhoo, that's not why we are writing today. We have your teeth. That's right, the ones you pawned and went back to get later, but they had been sold.

But don't you fret, we're more than happy to sell them back to you at a reasonable price. That reasonable price is $350,000, which includes $300K for the teeth plus a $50K finder's fee. Too high? Fine, enjoy your soup and Jell-O.

Ah, so nice to see that you have changed your mind. Please send a cashier's check to the address herein and we'll get these chompers right out to ya. That is, after you agree to one more stipulation.

We want you to stop making movies. You heard us. Just stop. You've made enough movies. It's time to retire. Get yourself a nice little spread up in Nutjob County and live out your days arguing with the voices in your head and wrestling mountain lions without a helmet.

We look forward to your reply.

Yours in dickery,

S. Finkter

55

SPECIPAN URINE HAT COMMODE SPECIMEN COLLECTION SYSTEM

LOCATION:

Unspecified (USA)

COST:

$1.95

DESCRIPTION:

The Kendall CURITY SPECIPAN Urine Hat Commode Specimen Collection System may be used as a urine collector, stool collector, or catch for kidney stones. Featuring easy-to-read calibrations, the Kendall CURITY SPECIPAN Urine Hat Commode Specimen Collection System fits inside your toilet.

Like our new cowboy hat? It's a bit stiff right now, but it will loosen up and get more comfy after we wear it about, oh, 350,000 times, give or take. But first we have to figure out how to get rid of that urine smell.

Okay, so it's not really a hat. It's a Specipan Urine Hat Commode Specimen Collection System, and that's a lot of names for a simple chunk of plastic. But then, "piss pot" would have been too easy and doesn't quite capture the nuances of this clever device.

How does it work? You put this thing in your toilet and pee or poop into it (not both, please), then give it to your doctor and say, "Happy birthday!" Hey, he asked for a sample!

That's it, that's all it does. But then, what else are you going to use to deliver an excrement sample to your doctor? A Tupperware bowl? Ziploc bag? Empty Pringles can? Have fun fishing your poop out of the toilet water by hand. It's harder than it looks, even with tongs.

See? You need Specipan. We all do. And if you never need it for a bathroom sample, Specipan makes a great mixing bowl thanks to the handy measurements on the inside wall.

CRAP THAT SCARES THE CRAP OUT OF US

FRIGHTENING, VILE, AND DOWNRIGHT CREEPY

We've seen a lot of weird stuff in our day, from an old woman picking up a dead opossum off a country road to cook for supper, to an airplane making an emergency landing on the freeway ahead of us, hitting a car, and bursting into flames. It takes a lot to scare us—and these items scare us. Maybe it's not so much the items as the fact that somebody actually came up with these things, made them, and now they want to sell them to others on eBay. Most frightening of all? People buy them.

56

BRISTOL STOOL CHART CIGARETTE CASE

LOCATION:

Upper Midwest, USA

COST:

$9.99

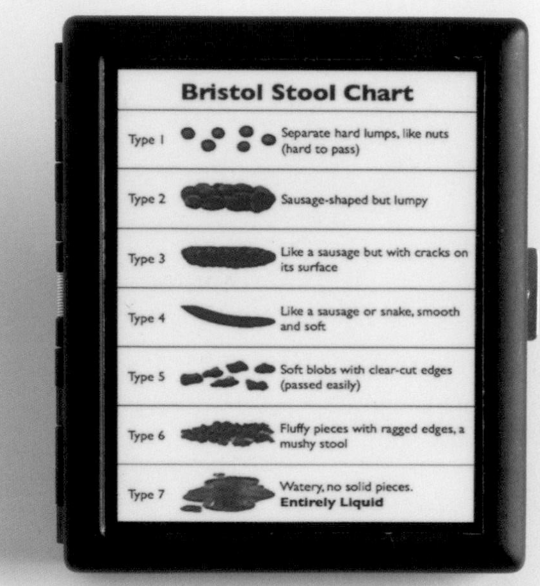

DESCRIPTION:

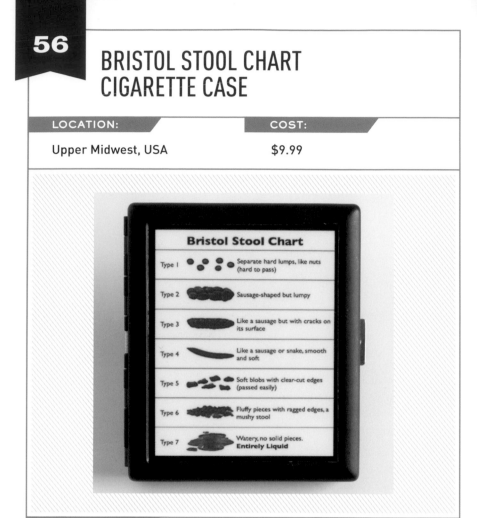

This is an awesome D.I.Y. business card holder, ID case, wallet, or cigarette case that is handmade by me and brand new. It is solid metal and black. It is lightweight and easy to carry around. Inside the case is enough room for those easy to lose track of items like your driver's license, student id, credit cards, cash, coins, etc., or it can fit two rows of 10 smokes each for a total of 20 regular sized cigarettes. Makes a great gift.

If you aren't familiar with the Bristol Stool Chart, you're in for a real treat. The chart, also known as the Bristol Stool Form Scale or the *North American Field Guide to Wild Turds*, is a medical guide for classifying various types of human feces in order to determine if your colon is healthy and squeezing out nice, beefy bowl-chokers. The scale identifies seven different types of crap, ranging from the hard little Milk Dud-like balls associated with constipation to the total liquid diarrhea associated with tequila and Arby's.

What makes the Bristol Chart so delightful is the creative way the authors, a team of gastroenterologists at the University of Bristol (UK), choose to describe shit. For example, Type 1 poo isn't just hard lumps, but "hard lumps *like nuts*." Type 4 turds are "*like sausage or a snake*, smooth and soft." The loose stool in Type 6 is brilliantly identified as "fluffy," and so on.

You'll note that four of the seven descriptions compare shit to food, appropriately enough, and three compare it to sausage. If you've ever eaten authentic English food, this comparison shouldn't surprise you.

There is, however, one glaring omission. We think the chart should include the kind of black, tarlike poop that makes you wish you had a bidet after you use an entire roll of TP and still don't get your cornhole completely clean. This type would fall between Types 1 and 2 on the chart, and we would describe it this way: "Dark and sticky, like warm Nutella or licorice paste."

If you're wondering what a shit chart has to do with a card case, don't look at us. We don't make this crap, we only buy it and make fun of it. The seller suggests using it for your business cards, but we don't think handing out cards from a case covered with pictures of dookie will land you that dream job—or any job at all. Unless you're looking for plumbing work.

57

DR. G. H. MICHEL'S RESTOR SKIN® (SOFT BEIGE)

LOCATION: Sugar Notch, PA

COST: $4 + shipping

DESCRIPTION:

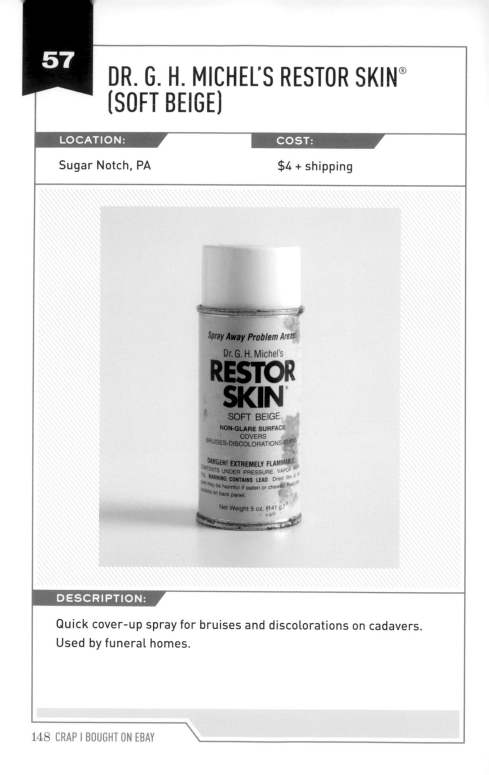

Quick cover-up spray for bruises and discolorations on cadavers. Used by funeral homes.

We've all seen (and made fun of) things like spray-on hair and tan-in-a-can, right? But Restor Skin® is no ordinary beauty product, and it's not the kind of thing you'll find on the Revlon display at Walgreens.

No, Restor Skin® is a specialty product made for a narrowly defined and uniquely demanding target market: the six-feet-under crowd. You know, individuals who have assumed room temperature. That's right: Restor Skin® is for dead people. Corpses. Cadavers. Stiffs. And not just any stiffs, but ones who get a little, well, dinged up on their way to the Other Side.

Morticians use it to "spray away problem areas" like "burns, discolorations, and bruises." One assumes these things aren't so much problem areas for the dead person—he has more pressing issues—but for loved ones who, for whatever reason, feel the need to take one last peek at him before he gets planted in the ground.

The seller tells us he found the can rolling around in the back of a used hearse he bought, which suggests that morticians keep this stuff handy at all times for those last-minute touch-ups, Aqua Net-style. "Crap, I can still see the bullet holes. Give him another spritz of this."

Picture two guys in suits in the back of a hearse, one keeping a lookout for family members while the other sprays this shit on some poor dead sap's face until he starts looking like a cross between Nosferatu and Bette Davis in *Whatever Happened to Baby Jane?*

Yet another reason to be cremated.

58

VULVA—NATURAL FEMALE SCENT

LOCATION:

Franklin, NH

COST:

$20

DESCRIPTION:

Vulva Original is a scented product with a vaginal odor that is specifically described as not being a perfume. The scent is intended to stimulate the wearer rather than someone else. While most perfume products act as "odor cues" and are used to improve one's personal odor in order to become more attractive or socially acceptable, Vulva Original is designed to be consumed by its owner by applying a drop of it to skin for sniffing it immediately after.

Panty-sniffers, this is your lucky day! Forget about sneaking into your girlfriend's dirty laundry hamper or lingering around the Nautilus equipment at the gym to get your fix. Who has time for those kinds of shenanigans? Now you can inhale the delightful bouquet of sweaty lady bits wherever and whenever your perverted little heart desires.

At first when we saw this, we assumed that it was a cologne—disturbing enough on its own—but no. When we found out what it's really for, its nasty factor reached a whole 'nother level. You see, it's not meant to make the wearer smell like a vag while out and about in the world; it's meant for people to dab on themselves and sniff because they enjoy the delicate scent of dirty panties. To which we reply: ew.

Still, we wonder what this stuff could possibly smell like. Are we talking about just-showered girl parts, just ran a marathon girl parts, or something in between? Before we spent our twenty hard-earned dollars, we decided to ask the seller.

↗ Dear CrotchSweat,

How would you describe how this stuff smells?

S. Finkter

We were prepared for a snarky response to our stupid question, but he was very polite.

↗ Dear S. Finkter,

It smells like . . . the name. Strange I know . . . but fascinating.

Check out the website www.smellmeand.com for complete details. It isn't cologne in the conventional sense.

CrotchSweat

Of course, we went straight to the website and were treated to a commercial of a man and a woman in a gym. She's sweating profusely and riding a stationary bike as he admires her sexy physique. There's about a minute of slow-motion close-ups of her perspiring body before she finishes her workout and heads for the showers. That's when the man ambles over and oh-so-casually sniffs her bicycle seat. He sniffs her bicycle seat, people!

Just let that sink in for a moment. Every fear you've ever had about that creepy guy at the gym is true. Apparently, there are so many people in this world who enjoy the scent of your nether regions that someone decided to bottle the aroma and sell it on eBay. The good news is that Creepy Gym Dude can buy it, too, so maybe your bicycle seat is safe, after all.

59

BLACK LEATHER DOG MASK HOOD

LOCATION:	COST:
St. Petersburg, FL	$34.99

DESCRIPTION:

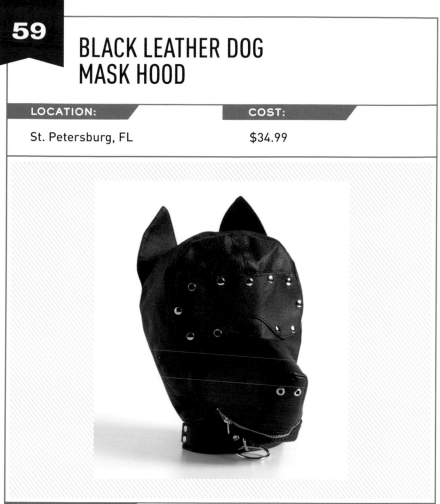

Sit. Stay. Bark. Designed to have a dog style appearance, this mask fits easily over the whole head and uses a belt buckle style closure at the back. A tie up the back of the head allows for additional fitting and comfort for the wearer. The hood sports a D-ring in the front of the collar for attachment to a leash. There is a zipper closure at the mouth. Eye covering can also be removed and snapped back on. Made of PU Leather.

Maybe it's us, but we can't look at this mask without hearing the *Scooby-Doo* theme song in our heads and thinking about Shaggy wearing this thing while getting whipped into submission with a riding crop by a leather-clad Velma.

SMACK!
Shaggy: "Zoinks! Like, ow, man."

We're not really experts at S&M. Sure, who hasn't had their bum spanked while wearing a ball gag, fur handcuffs, and anal beads? But beyond that, we're clueless. One of you hard-core deviants needs to tell us what this mask is all about. You wear it when you want to be treated like a dog? Why not just go to Neiman-Marcus or the DMV like the rest of us?

Cary came home one day to his daughter wearing this mask, which might have been funny had it not been so disturbing. Who wants to see a fourth-grader in bondage gear? (Don't answer that.) Luckily, she thought it was a Halloween costume.

"Why is Scooby-Doo's mouth zipped up?" she asked.

"Um," said Cary, thinking fast. "So he won't eat so many Scooby snacks."

"Oh. Good idea. He's getting fat." And off she went.

Then Cary hid all the rest of the crap we bought on eBay. God forbid she start asking questions about the rubber sex doll or the whacking tube.

60

POOP-SHAPED SOAP (PLAIN OR WITH CORN)

LOCATION:

Bradenton, FL

COST:

$17.96

DESCRIPTION:

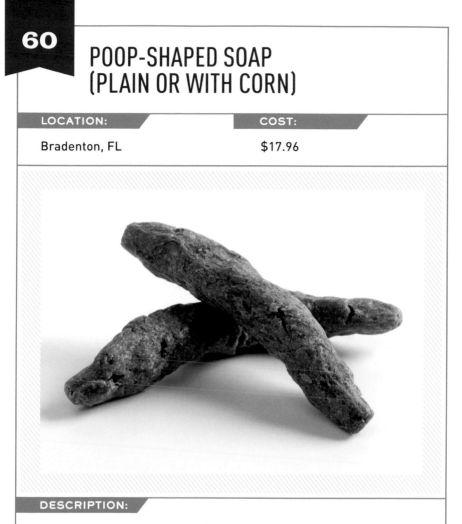

Sure to cause outrageous bathroom double-takes! Completely usable poop soaps smell great but look like genuine you-know-whats! Soaps are about 6" long each. Vary slightly in sizes, shapes, and colors. Set of 2, one plain poop and one corn poop.

We are both parents of young kids, so walking into a bathroom and seeing a turd lying by the sink is sadly not the most outrageous (or infrequent) thing that's ever happened to us. In fact, considering the number of times we've each had to scrub poop off the wall or rinse diarrhea out of a pair of Spiderman underwear, we didn't think anyone could scare us with poop. *Ever*.

Until now. Check out this awesome soap that looks like two good-sized bowl-chokers. We love how you can get your turds with or without corn niblets, just like the real deal after eating at Popeye's Chicken. Speaking of Popeye's, we wonder if this soap comes in liquid form.

We actually love this soap; then again, we're admittedly very immature. As soon as these flowery-smelling Lincoln Logs arrived in the mail, we started brainstorming funny things to do with them. Adding some floaters to someone's bath might be fun, or making a point of washing your hands with it in front of your dinner guests right before handling their food. Maybe simply place it in the guest bathroom when the in-laws visit?

We decided to test them out by leaving them in the toilet at work. When people complained about the unflushed mess, we plucked them out of the bowl with our bare hands and stifled a giggle as they gasped in horror. We sniffed the poop, and, in our best Bill Murray in *Caddyshack* voice, said, "It's no big deal."

It's okay, we didn't like that job anyway. Hopefully the people at our next job will have a better sense of humor.

61

ISRAELI MILITARY GAS MASK

LOCATION:

Sullivan, MO

COST:

$16.50

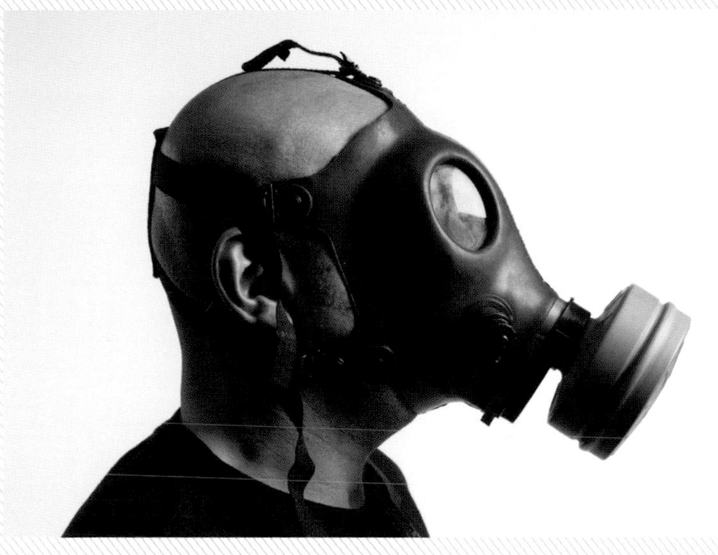

DESCRIPTION:

Adult Rubber Gas Mask with Adjustable Head Straps. Includes Hose, New Filter and Drinking Tube. New Israeli army item. Includes Additional Side Filter and Drinking tube not shown in photo. You Can drink while wearing gas mask. Real working gas mask or Scary costume accessory. Hose can be removed or a filter put in its place.

Before we talk About This mask, can we just Say how much We love Random word capitalization? Properly Capitalized copy is So boring and predictable.

If you're wondering why the Israeli army is selling off their gas masks on eBay, so are we. Things must be getting better in the Middle East; that, or they got better ones and are dumping these off on eBay suckers, just like when your older sister drives the wheels off her car and then it's bequeathed to you like some great prize, but it's really crap, and you're the one who ends up stranded in Cornhole, USA, at three a.m. because she never changed the oil. Oil? What's that?

If you don't anticipate needing a gas mask anytime soon, you can always try these:

1. Beer Bong: Someone pours a giant beer down the tube, but instead of going right down your throat, the beer fills up the mask and you have to drink it before you drown. Your friends can watch the beer level slowly descend in the eyeholes as you chug for your life. Or they can watch you die. Either way, they are entertained, and if you must die doing something, making others laugh isn't a bad way to go.
2. Bong: We won't condone smoking dope, but if you're already a pothead, here's a way to enjoy massive bong hits while looking totally bitchin' doing it, Cheech. Talk about a hot box. You'll inhale whether you want to or not, and get totally baked in no time. Then when you get all paranoid and shit from the pot, the mask will hide your face from all those people who are staring at you and totally know how stoned you are.

For those of you past your partying years and starting a family, the mask will come in handy at poopy-diaper-changing-time, because—this just in—baby shit is foul. We realize that changing your kid's diaper while wearing a gas mask may frighten him—it could very well scar him for life, causing him to have bonding issues, PTSD, low self-esteem, and a fear of the Israeli army—but it can't be any worse than watching you turn green and choke back vomit every time you open this recently befouled diaper. Mmm. Fresh from the oven.

ADULTS-ONLY CRAP

WASH BEFORE USING

If you ever wished you could turn back the clock to a time before you knew what things like a dildo or jizz or double inputs were, this chapter will only make it worse. Here, just for you, we've cooked up a big pot of Lurid and Prurient in the form of some of the creepiest, nastiest, what-the-fuck-iest sex toys you ever saw. These are things no one should ever have to see, but we show them to you anyway so that you can fully comprehend the levels of depravity and bad taste all around us. If you already own any of these, do us all a favor: get some help.

62

I (HEART) JIZZ RAGS

LOCATION: Sin City, USA

COST: $2.49

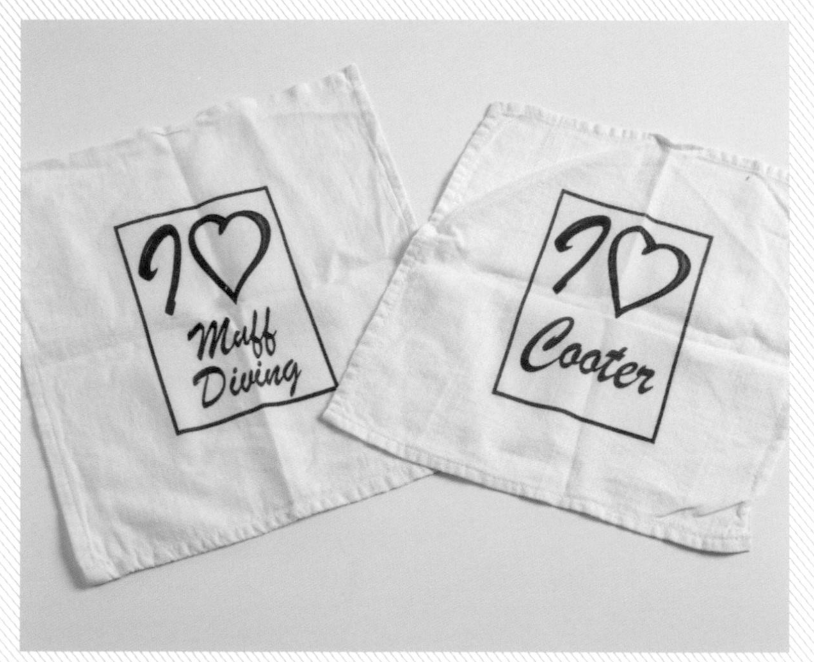

DESCRIPTION:

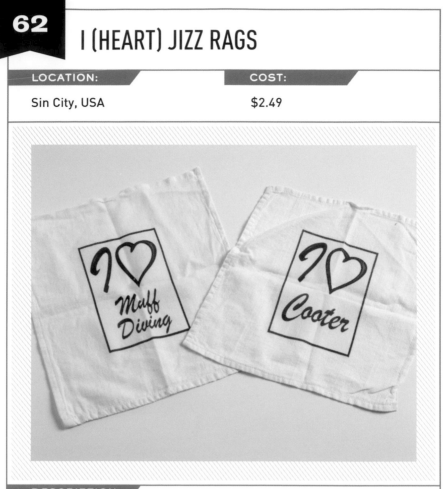

Tired of using your favorite t-shirt to clean up jizz? Can't remember which towel you used till you accidentally wipe your face with your used jizz rag? Yuk! Don't do that anymore! You need a designated jizz rag. Now you can get one personalized with whatever you like, or choose from one of our existing ones. White/100% Cotton/12" × 12"

"You need a designated jizz rag." The man has a point. We do need a jizz rag, though not as badly as some people, apparently. We've never been so desperate to clean up a post-wank mess that we used a favorite shirt. Not one of our own, at least. (Sorry, Dad.)

The jizz rag seller has a huge selection on eBay, so choosing which preprinted spunk towels we wanted wasn't easy. We finally narrowed it down to three, including "I (Heart) 69" and "I (Heart) My Big White Cock," but in the end we chose "I (Heart) Muff Diving," probably because we've always enjoyed the visual quality of that phrase. We also purchased a personalized jizz rag, so we contacted the seller with instructions.

↗ Dear JizzRagJohnny:

I just purchased a personalized jizz rag from you. Can you put anything I want on it?

Thanks,

S. Finkter

↗ Dear S. Finkter,

Yes, whatever text you like as long as it fits on the rag.

JizzRagJohnny

↗ Dear JizzRagJohnny,

Great. Make my jizz rag read, "I (heart) Pomeranians." A little unorthodox, I realize, but they do turn me on. I just wish they were easier to catch. Also, they bite.

S. Finkter

↗ Dear S. Finkter,

I'm sorry, I cannot write anything illegal on the jizz rags. Please choose different text.

JizzRagJohnny

↗ Dear JizzRagJohnny,

What's illegal about liking Pomeranians? I'm not saying I have sex with them. (I'm not saying I don't, either . . . heh heh.) But whatever. Just put "I (Heart) My Sister" instead.

S. Finkter

↗ Dear S. Finkter,

Maybe I'm not being clear. Incest is illegal, too. I can't do it. Pick something legal, please.

JizzRagJohnny

↗ Dear JizzRagJohnny,

What happened to "any text you want"? I don't plug my sister. I just think about her sometimes when I touch myself. Is that a crime? She's my stepsister anyway.

S. Finkter

↗ Dear S. Finkter,

Cut the shit and tell me what you want on the rag or I will cancel the sale. I don't make enough money on these to put up with bullshit.

JizzRagJohnny

Testy, testy! Sounds like someone needs a wank himself. He's all uptight and stuff.

↗ Dear JizzRagJohnny,

Fine. Put "I (Heart) Having My Balls Gargled by DoucheRag Johnny" on it.

S. Finkter

↗ Dear S. Finkter,

You would like that, wouldn't you?

JizzRag Johnny

We never got our personalized towel, in case you were wondering.

63

CYBERSKIN LOVE DOLL W/ 2 ENTRIES, 2 VIBRATORS

LOCATION: Emeryville, CA

COST: $59.99

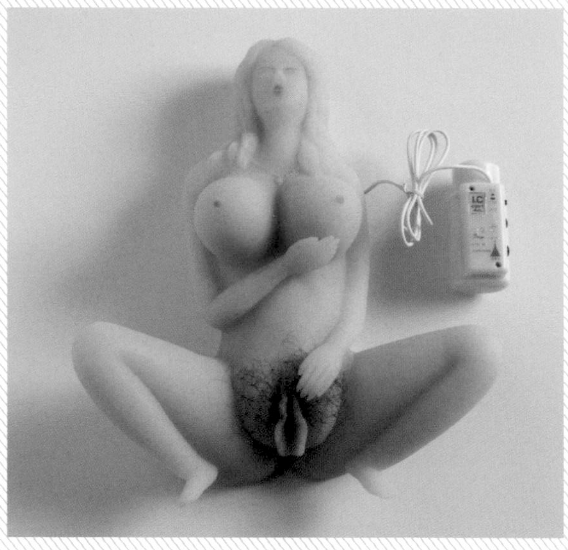

DESCRIPTION:

Super Realistic; Solid Love Doll
1 Throbber and 1 Vibrator with Multi-speed Controllers
2 Cavities, Vaginal and Anal
All Allow Deep Insertions
The Ultimate Experience in Stimulation!
Vibrating bullet brings you strong pulse as hard as you like
Multi-speed throbbing gives you real sexual action
Both entries are 9" in depth
Weight: 4 lb

Remember the scene in *This Is Spinal Tap* when the band expects a life-sized model of Stonehenge to appear on stage, but instead of twelve feet tall, the model is twelve inches tall and "in danger of being trampled by dwarves"? That's how we felt when we opened the Cyberskin Love Doll: a little (pun intended) underwhelmed.

It's not that the seller didn't explain the dimensions in his listings; he did. We just didn't pay attention. We were too mesmerized by that pubic hair. Right now, somewhere in Turkey, a YMCA shower drain is missing its hairball.

But hey, it's not all bad. Our girl is soft, she's squishy, and she has some tig ol' bitties that jiggle like crazy when you play Hacky Sack with her or throw her for a touchdown. Her best feature, however, her pièce de résistance, is that bigger-than-life vajingo. Holy crap! That woman with nineteen kids? She's got nothing on this gal.

Someday this beauty will make a lonely guy who can't get real nookie very happy, as long as he can pretend he's banging a real woman and not a badger.

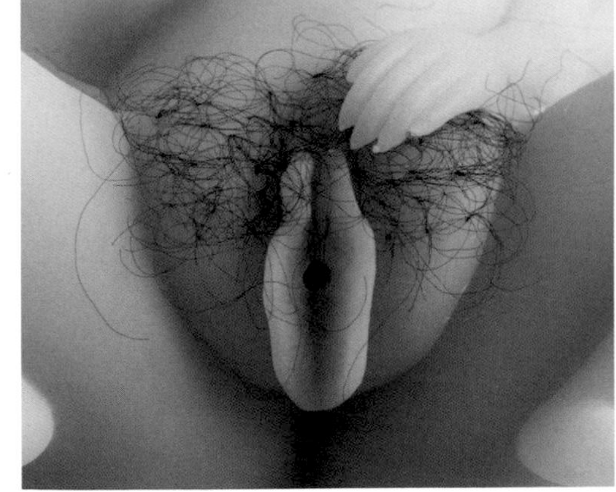

Also makes a great pencil sharpener!

64

PENIS ENLARGEMENT: SUBLIMINAL MESSAGE CD

LOCATION:	COST:
New York, NY	$4.95

DESCRIPTION:

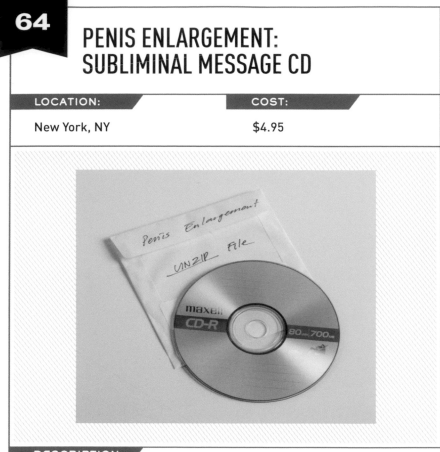

This CD was developed by numerous Medical Doctors and PhDs in psychiatry and psychology. This CD-R has seven classical music files where the subliminal messages are blended together in sound frequencies (Hz) that are NOT audible to the conscious mind but ARE audible to the subconscious mind. You will feel that you are simply listening to the good old classical music, but your SUBconscious mind will continuously receive the subliminal messages that are mixed together (in specific frequencies) with high tech mixing devices.

Who knew that the key to having a bigger unit lies within the gray matter between your ears? We feel like Dorothy finding out that she had the power to go back to Kansas all along!

According to this seller, all you need to do to add more "Dirk" to your "Diggler" is listen to this soothing CD of classical music. Hidden within the music is a subliminal message that will somehow convince your brain to increase your penis size. Right. And our bank accounts will also fill with money if we think hard enough.

↗ Dear Mungo Cojones,

How do subliminal messages make the penis bigger? How many inches can we expect? You say the CD just sounds like classical music, so I am hoping that I can play these CDs and make my husband's unit bigger without him realizing it. Is that possible?

S. Finkter

↗ Dear S. Finkter,

Yes, your husband won't realize why he is having larger size, as he will just listen to classical music. Usually, the increment is about 1 to 2 inches depending on the person. As an average, 1.5 inches. This CD will increase sex drive by constantly providing with erotic messages.

Mungo

When we started playing this CD around the house, the craziest stuff happened. The old man's wang didn't change a bit, but his balls expanded like two ripe grapefruits. He could barely sit, and seeing him in a pair of khakis gave new meaning to the term "moose knuckle."

The doctors were stumped, but we knew what had caused it: subliminal messages. That may also be what caused the lady of the house to grow a beard and the cat to start humping on the dog like it's his job. Blame it on the Bach.

65

THE ACCOMMODATOR ORAL SEX ENHANCER

LOCATION:	COST:
New Jersey, USA	$26

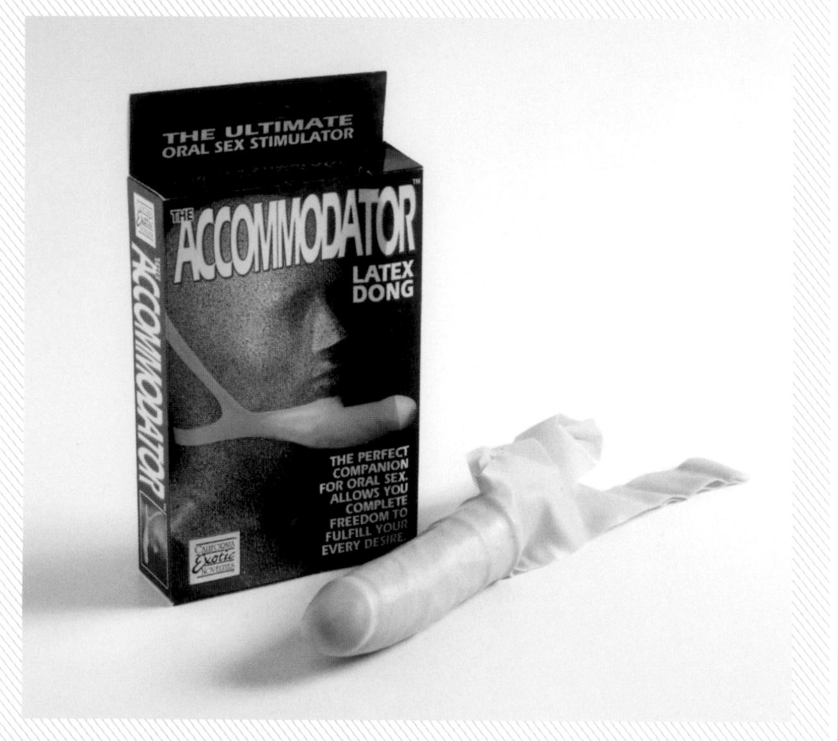

DESCRIPTION:

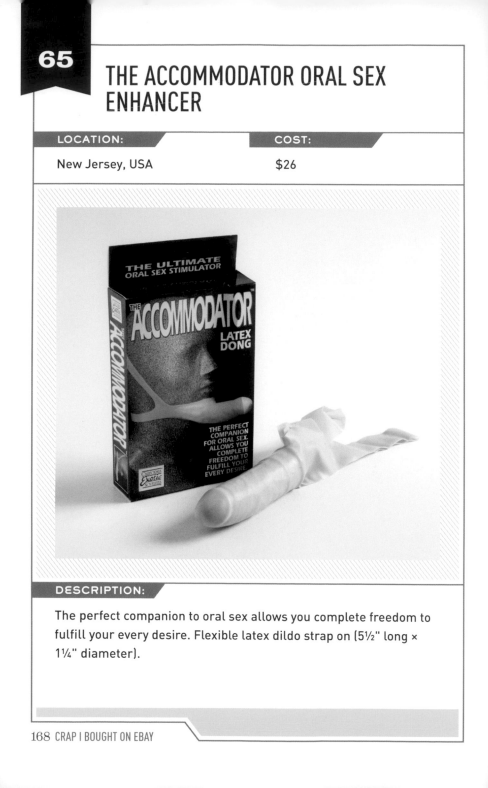

The perfect companion to oral sex allows you complete freedom to fulfill your every desire. Flexible latex dildo strap on (5½" long × 1¼" diameter).

Ladies and germs, we present to you The Accommodator, a handy little gadget that may very well be our favorite item in this entire book. Why? Because it's the most ridiculous goddamn thing we've ever seen, that's why. Look at it. Seriously. WTF?

If you're wondering what it does—other than look preposterous—the eBay seller calls it "the perfect companion to oral sex." No, the perfect companion to oral sex is someone *giving* you oral sex; this is a rubber dildo you wear on your head so that you can pleasure your partner in two ways at once. We'll let you do the math.

"But wait," you're saying, "I can already do that without The Accommodator." Perhaps, but The Accommodator also leaves your hands free to do other things, like make spaghetti or trade stocks online.

The only problem with this multitasking marvel is that it looks like a cross between a slingshot and orthodontic headgear. It may feel great to the person being "accommodated," but you have to wonder how they can watch you use it without crying tears of hysterical laughter.

The trick, we can only assume—because there's no way in hell either of us is touching this thing—is to close your eyes and pretend you aren't being violated by Jay Leno.

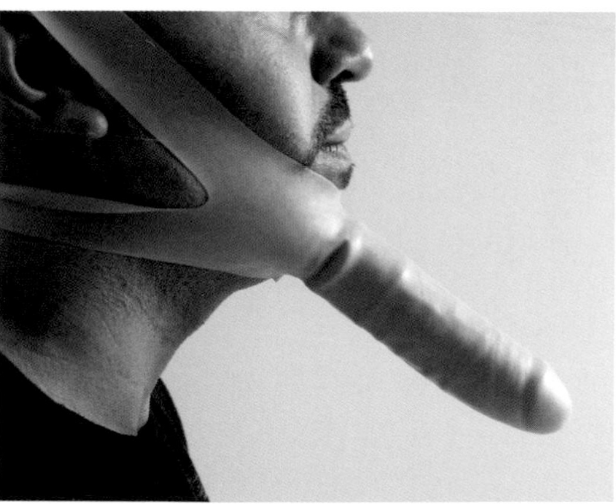

66

WATERPROOF CHASTITY BELT— FEMALE DEVICE

LOCATION: Shanghai, China

COST: $16.99

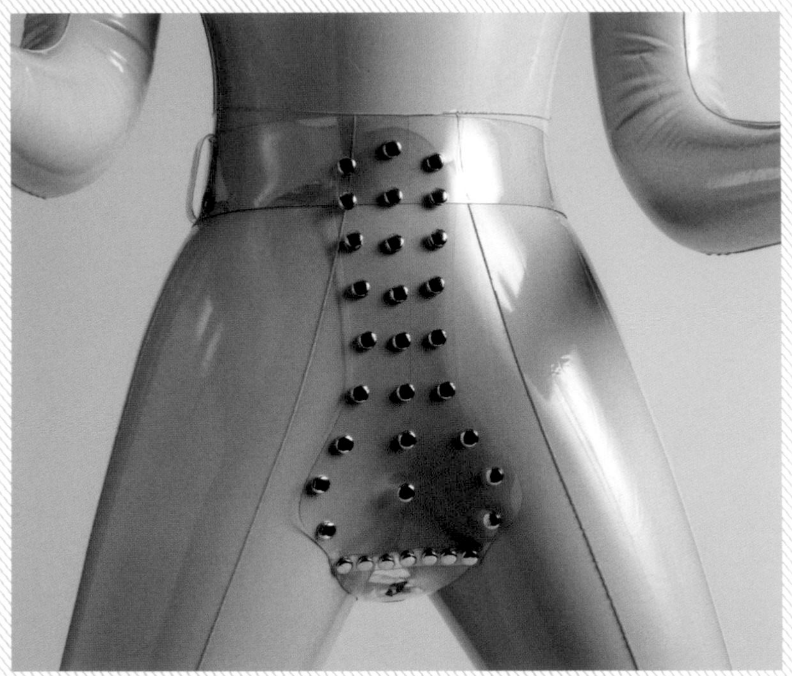

DESCRIPTION:

Chastity Belt Device. Water Proof Material. You can take bath or swim with It!!! Come With Lock & Keys. Custom Accessory Item. Extremely Cool & Sexy!!! Brand New. Transparent. High quality, soft real cowskin leather. Size: Can be adjusted to Fit All People.

We can always tell when a seller doesn't speak what we would call fluent English, and not just because they happen to live in Shanghai.

First of all, when we got our chastity belt in the mail, it was obvious that there's no way in hell it would fit "all people"; maybe all Chinese people, but definitely not all morbidly obese Quarter Pounder-eating Americans.

Then we noticed that this chastity belt is made of plastic, so we're thinking "cowskin leather" is either ~~a big fat lie~~ an exaggeration, or an example of something getting lost in translation. Either that or there are some kind of transparent cows out there that we're not aware of. Surely what the seller meant to say was, "This contraption is made out of metal and plastic and is guaranteed to chafe you in all of your most sensitive spots."

It looks uncomfortable, but if it's really a chastity belt, it may come in handy. Got a relative in a nursing home? Let's keep the creepy night janitor out of her lady business the old-fashioned way: slap a chastity belt on her! Got a daughter whose hormones are pushing her toward a future on MTV's *Teen Mom*? Chastity belt. Going out of town and leaving behind your girlfriend, a known slut? Chastity belt that bitch!

↗ **Dear Unhappy Ending,**

Does this device really keep out cock? Looks kind of flimsy.

S. Finkter

↗ **Dear Finkster,**

Close enough.

This is for woman. Not sure if it can be worn by man.

Unhappy Ending

Hm. See what we mean about the English issues?

67

ROAD WARRIOR WHACKER MASTURBATOR

LOCATION: Los Angeles, CA

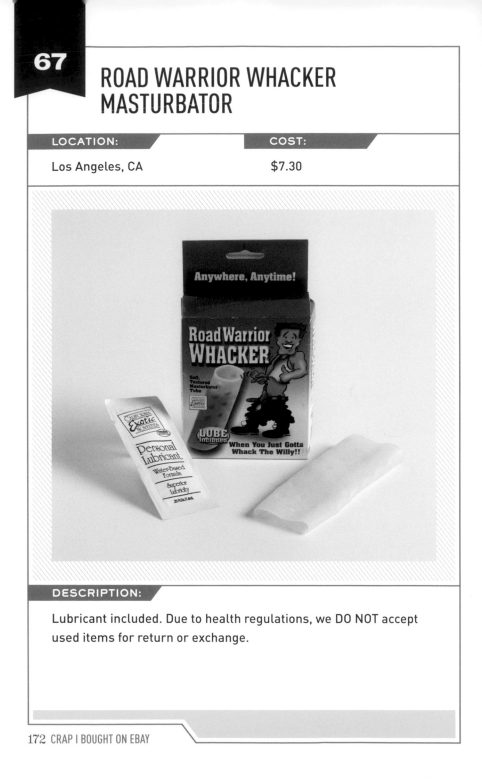

COST: $7.30

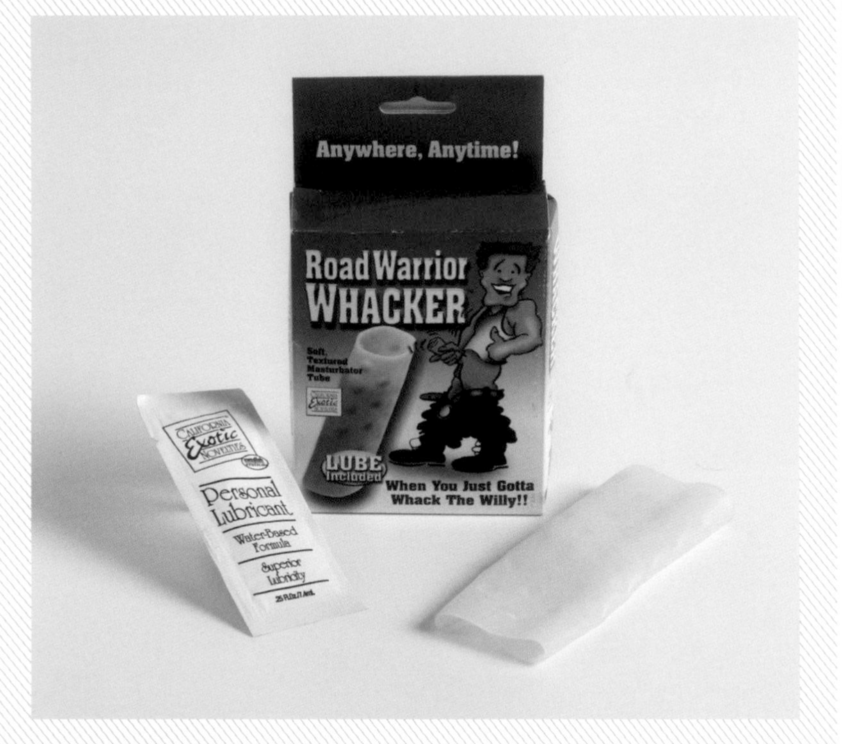

Anywhere, Anytime!
Road Warrior WHACKER
Soft, Textured Masturbator Tube
LUBE Included
When You Just Gotta Whack The Willy!!
California Exotic Novelties
Personal Lubricant
Water-Based Formula
Superior Lubricity

DESCRIPTION:

Lubricant included. Due to health regulations, we DO NOT accept used items for return or exchange.

Here's a handy little knickknack to grab if you want to get arrested or crash your car and burn to death inside with your pants around your ankles and your dick in your hand.

The Road Warrior Whacker is a nubbed rubber cylinder that you carry around in case you're out and about and suddenly overcome with an urge to pleasure yourself *immediately*. When you gotta spank, you gotta spank, so why exercise decorum and wait until you get home?

Just drop your drawers like the little creep on the package front, whip out the RWW, and rub one out "anywhere, anytime," as the box says: in church, in court, at your kid's soccer game, in a meeting with the boss, at the bus stop, or any other time you "just gotta whack the willy." So what if you go to jail? You can use it there, too, but be prepared to share, because once your fellow inmates see the Road Warrior in action, they will want a turn.

Is this product really necessary? We posed that very question to our seller.

↗ Dear Spankmonger,

I am intrigued by the product, but I can see no real reason to purchase it. Why use this when I can get the same results with my hand, which I don't have to carry around with me because it's attached to my arm?

S. Finkter

↗ Dear S. Finkter,

I don't suppose it is a whole lot different except this item is textured inside, so it is a bit more stimulating than your hand.

Spankmonger

↗ Dear Spankmonger,

My hand is pretty textured inside, too. Lots of calluses on my palms, if you know what I mean heh heh ;)

S. Finkter

↗ Dear S. Finkter,

Disgusting.

Spankmonger

Disgusting? She's selling jerkoff tubes on eBay and *we're* disgusting?

CRAP FOR YOUR CRITTERS

BECAUSE PETS CAN'T SAY NO

They give us unconditional love and devotion. What do we give them in return? Crap. By the boatload. Who knows why we torture our poor innocent animals with humiliation and awkward intimacy in clothing a dead blind man wouldn't be caught wearing. Perhaps because we can; it's not like they can say no. Karma is a bitch on wheels, though, and we had better pray that there is no such thing as reincarnation, especially if we are the kind of pet owners who foist upon our poor animals the kind of products you're about to see in this chapter.

Because there will be a reckoning.

CANINE SEMEN COLLECTION SLEEVES

LOCATION: USA

COST: $5.99

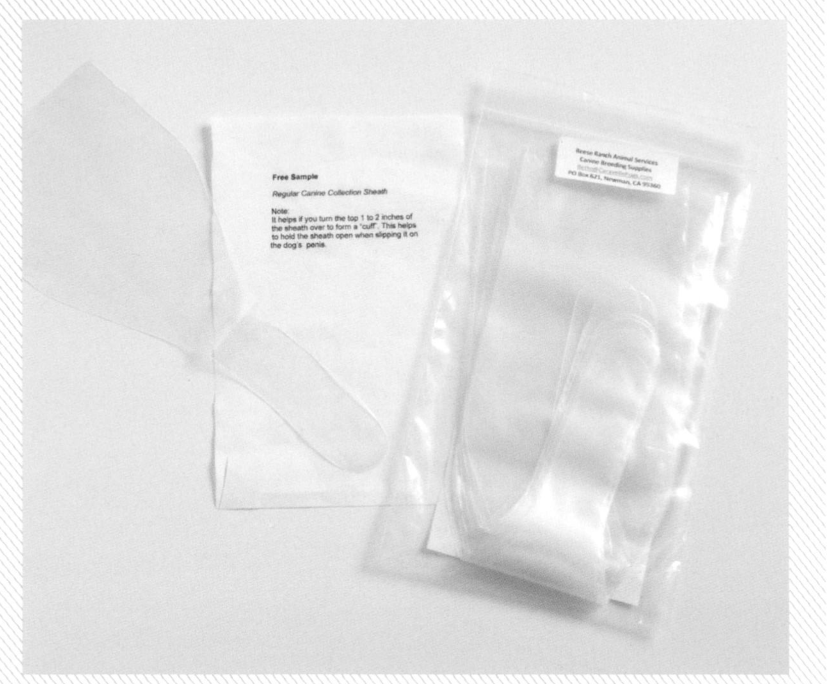

DESCRIPTION:

Ten Pack of Super Soft Canine Semen Collection Sleeves or Sheaths. These are disposable, one-piece sheaths for collecting a dog's semen in order to perform an AI (artificial insemination) on the bitch or to collect canine semen to ship. Instructions included.

File this one under: Things We Never Want to Think About. EVER.

Yes, we are aware of the fact that dog breeders have to retrieve doggy spoo in order to artificially knock up da bitches, but we really, really, *really* don't want to think about how that particular magic happens. Until this moment, we thought breeders simply locked two fertile dogs in a room with some Boone's Farm Apple Wine and let nature take its course, kind of like prom.

But no. Apparently they have to . . . *ugh* . . . retrieve it. We wonder who gets the honor of jerking off their dog into these handy sterile sheaths. Thankfully for that unlucky person, the sheaths come with detailed instructions on how to curl your dog's toes with just a few gentle tugs of the ol' doggy dong.

We briefly wondered how one goes about getting a dog in "the mood"; maybe give him a copy of *Dog Fancy* or a calendar of poodles wearing tutus or something? Then we decided that we really don't want to know how one summons a pooch's pink lipstick. Heck, you can probably buy dog spunk on eBay anyway, thereby saving yourself the hassle of introducing Fido to Rosie Palm and her five daughters!

We decided not to search eBay for dog semen, though. We may never be able to look our dog in the eye again as it is.

Free Sample

Regular Canine Collection Sheath

Note:
It helps if you turn the top 1 to 2 inches of the sheath over to form a "cuff". This helps to hold the sheath open when slipping it on the dog's penis.

69

FEMALE DOG SANITARY DIAPER/PANTS

LOCATION:

Hong Kong, China

COST:

$4.73

DESCRIPTION:

Elastic belt with plastic button is detachable. Paw pattern pet pants looks very cute and attractive.

Every woman knows that wearing a maxi pad does feel a bit like wearing a diaper, but imagine if you had to wear it outside your clothes so everyone around you knew you were on the rag. We just had a few quick questions for our seller.

↗ Dear Florence Catcher,

I'm thinking of getting one of these for my dog. She really hates the tampons I've been using on her. What size should I order for a 70 lb. pit bull?

S. Finkter

↗ Dear S. Finkter,

This is only for small dogs. 10 lbs. or less. Thank you.

Flo

↗ Dear Flo,

Darn! What should I do about my dog's periods, then? Things are getting really gross and messy up in here.

S. Finkter

↗ Dear S. Finkter,

I don't know. Maybe if I find bigger diaper I will email you.

Flo

Is she blowing us off? Not cool, Flo. Not cool.

↗ Dear Flo,

Yes, please do email me. I might want to try some of these myself. Will they fit a human?

S. Finkter

No response. I think Flo was either on to us or had just given up, not that we blame her. Didn't matter, though, because we found a solution that suits both us and our bleeding bitch: Depends and a pair of scissors.

70

CABLE-KNIT SCHOOLGIRL OUTFIT FOR DOGS

LOCATION:

Livingston, TX

COST:

$3.99

DESCRIPTION:

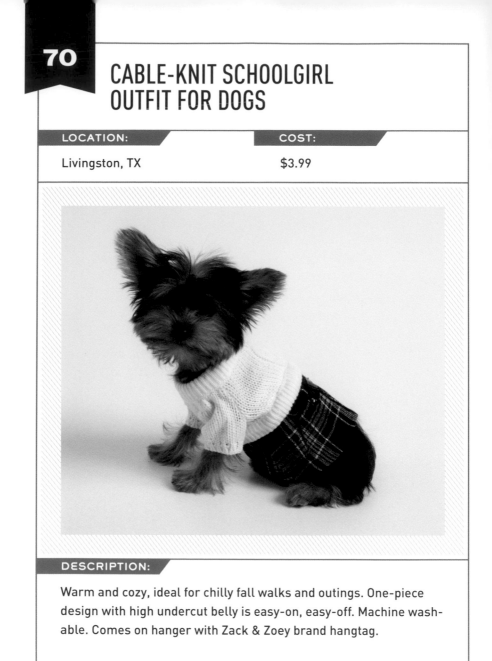

Warm and cozy, ideal for chilly fall walks and outings. One-piece design with high undercut belly is easy-on, easy-off. Machine washable. Comes on hanger with Zack & Zoey brand hangtag.

Very few people can rock a kilt without looking like a total twat. Burly Scottish men, Axl Rose, Catholic schoolgirls—definitely. You know who can never, ever pull off a kilt and cable-knit sweater combo without looking like an idiot? A dog.

Just imagine the abject shame and horror your pooch will experience when you dress her up like a wee schoolgirl in a kilt and make her stroll around the dog park in front of all her doggy friends. You'd best put aside some money for dog therapy later. And sleep with your bedroom door locked.

We've all seen people who put their little toy doggies in sweaters or rain jackets when it's chilly or wet, and sure, some of those tiny dogs really do need help, like the practically hairless ones who quiver and shake 24/7. But sometimes their owners aren't protecting their dogs from the elements, they're just plain dressing them up like dorky little dolls for the hell of it, and that just ain't right.

Not to mention the fact that this thing looks like something some kinky fetish freak with a schoolgirl fixation would force his dog into wearing. We're sure he tells his dog that she looks just like Britney Spears in her ". . . Baby One More Time" video, but he lies. The pervert.

Where is PETA when you need them? If humans aren't allowed to wear fur because it's cruel, shouldn't it be faux pas to dress your animal like jailbait?

There's a reason this outfit only comes in small and x-small: no self-respecting German shepherd would be caught dead in it. You could try putting it on them, but we don't recommend it if you want to keep all of your digits intact.

71

POOP FREEZE SPRAY (AEROSOL-FREE)

LOCATION: USA

COST: $10.99

DESCRIPTION:

POOP FREEZE is the first freeze-spray aerosol made for animal waste pick-up. Completely Non-flammable Cools surfaces down to -62 F. No CFCs to destroy the ozone. Does not harm vegetation. Can be used indoors or outdoors. Totally environmentally friendly. Spray. Wait 10 seconds and a white crusty film solidifies the waste. A Clean . . . Easy . . . Quick . . . Affordable solution to nasty waste clean-up problems.

We love dogs, but they are kind of gross, yes? They sniff each other's butts to say hello. They drink from the toilet, roll in animal carcasses, think garbage is a delicacy, and eat kitty-litter-encrusted cat turds like they're coconut macaroons.

That's something we all sign on for when we decide to include a dog in our lives; it's kind of an unwritten contract between man and beast. Dogs agree to love us unconditionally, be furry and adorable, and occasionally protect us from scary people like the mailman and that Jehovah's Witness knocking on your door. In return, we humans agree to feed them, bathe them, pet them, walk them, drop oodles of money on vet bills, and yes, clean up their piles of still-warm feces.

Most people just use a plastic grocery bag, but oh, no, not Princess. We wouldn't want her to have to acknowledge that she's one thin sheet of plastic away from having a big honkin' dog turd in her well-manicured hand, now would we?

↗ Dear Princess Ladyfingers,

Quick question: does this spray work on any other kinds of poop or is it canine-specific? I'm thinking this might make changing my toddler's diaper a lot less disgusting. Can I just spray it right on his bum?

S. Finkter

↗ Dear S. Finkter,

I wouldn't use this on human skin as it could cause burns. It's really just good to freeze the dog (or cat) poop so it's less gross to handle.

Princess

↗ Dear Princess,

Bummer. One more question: what if I spray it right on my dog's butt while he's pooping? Wouldn't that be neat? Might be kind of a cool effect, too, like when water freezes coming out of a hose.

S. Finkter

↗ Dear S. Finkter,

Again, I would not spray this on skin, animal or human. Just spray the poop itself for easy clean-up.

Princess

Yeah, yeah, we get it, Princess. No cool *Mr. Freeze Poop Art* for us, which is a real shame because we bet we could get a pretty good price for something like that on eBay. After all, some people will buy anything.

72

PET FRENZY BIRTHDAY HAT

LOCATION:	COST:
Pottstown, PA	$7

DESCRIPTION:

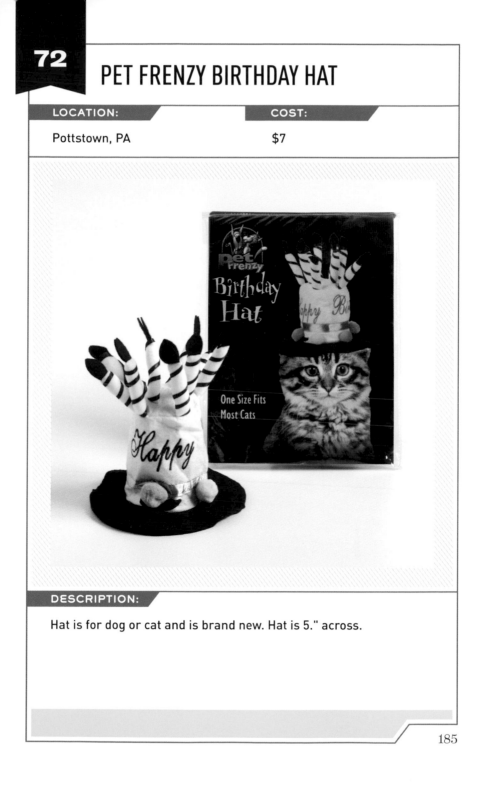

Hat is for dog or cat and is brand new. Hat is 5." across.

Hey look, it's a party hat for cats, because everyone knows that cats love to par-*tay*! Just feast your eyes on the startled cat on the package. We think the look on his face says it all, and that is: "OHMYGOD WHY AM I WEARING THIS RIDICULOUS HAT?!"

We know some people get a little weird about their pets, and that's totally understandable. Shut-ins and cat ladies need love too, after all. Yet there is a line, and we have to think that forcing your little dog or cat into a pompom and birthday candle-adorned felt party hat crosses that line by about a mile.

It's a well-known fact that cats are assholes. They could all be taken down a few notches just to show 'em who's boss, so maybe this party hat does serve some purpose. Plus, it could be worse: those could be real candles on top. If there's anything that cats love more than a rollicking good party, it's having fire attached to their heads.

We have known people who treat their pets like children, and not in a *good* way. We suggest skipping the silly hats and focusing on the important things, like keeping them fed and making sure they don't get rabies and kill someone. We think we'll all be a lot happier if we keep things simple.

73

MAGICKAL CAT CLAWS

LOCATION: Batesville, IN

COST: $0.99

DESCRIPTION:

This auction is for seven claws shed from a very magickal cat. Thanks for looking & please check out my other auctions!

We don't know what makes this cat "magickal" or why the owner thought selling his claws was a worthwhile use of time (or eBay), but that didn't stop us from snapping up this incredibly random item.

We're sorry, and we don't say this often, but what a stupid, ridiculous thing to sell. This seller must think we're complete idiots. A "magickal" cat? The only thing that's magical is that this guy got someone (us) to buy his useless cat's useless claws. Time to call shenanigans and ask this genius what's up.

↗ Dear MagiCat,

Why are these claws magical?

S. Finkter

↗ Dear S. Finkter,

The cat these claws came from is very magickal animal. He has a way of looking at u that makes u feel like he is reading ur mind. He brought us lots of good luck too.

MagiCat

↗ Dear MagiCat,

Am I supposed to eat them, wear them, or what?

S. Finkter

↗ Dear S. Finkter,

You can keep em in ur pocket for good luck. I wouldn't eat them. No.

MagiCat

Ha ha, now he tells us. The real question is: how good can this guy's luck be if he's selling cat claws on eBay for extra cash? Sounds like the same kind of luck that got that fake fortuneteller, Miss Cleo, sent to jail for being a big fat fraud. At least Miss Cleo's fake psychic readings made some people happy; this guy's crap just pissed us off and landed him a spot in a book about crazy crap on eBay.

CRAP ON WHEELS

CRAP FOR YOUR CRAPMOBILE

We've driven our fair share of crappy cars, but we've never added crap *to* our car . . . until now. In this chapter, you'll find an assortment of crazy items that are sure to transform your ride into a gen-u-ine moving violation and get you cited for Failure to Yield to Common Decency. Face it: it may not be illegal to have an incredibly raunchy bumper sticker or a toilet seat affixed to your trailer hitch, but it's definitely a crime against good taste.

74

OFF-ROAD COMMODE HITCH RECEIVER-MOUNTED TOILET SEAT NEW

LOCATION:	COST:
Fort Mill, SC	$39.99

DESCRIPTION:

Every sportsman needs his own throne, and the Off-Road Commode fits the bill—with comfort and luxury to boot! Easily attaches to any 2in. receiver hitch and supports up to 500 lbs. The 1-5⁄16in. dia. steel tube seat is covered with soft, padded camo. A great gift for hunting, fishing, and camping buddies! Not for use when vehicle is in motion.

Sometimes it's the little things that make life worth living: watching a punk teenager fall off his skateboard and break a limb; wearing your Grim Reaper costume into the smoking room at the airport; and using the great outdoors as your own personal toilet—which is why we adore the Off-Road Commode Hitch Receiver-Mounted Toilet Seat. Now, wherever you go, you can *go*. And that, friends, is what freedom is all about. God bless America.

We are glad this thing is NEW and not used, because you never know whose sweaty ass might have already been on it. The camo tends to hide stains, if you get our drift. We're also glad the seller pointed out that you shouldn't use the seat while the car is in motion, although if you suffer from constipation, such a scenario might help you.

With the ORCHRMTS, you can take road trips without worrying about finding a McDonald's or getting chloroformed and ass-raped at a public rest stop. Now, if you are cruising down the highway and are overcome with a sudden urge to evacuate your bowels RIGHT THIS INSTANT, all you have to do is pull over to the shoulder, drop your drawers, and let 'er rip.

"But wait, Bev and Cary," we hear you asking, "What about passing cars? Won't they see me? I can't go if someone is watching me."

Nope. The seat is camouflaged! You'll be virtually invisible as you drop that deuce. Best of all, the seat stays attached to your car, so once you're done leaving your calling card in the middle of the road or campsite, you can hop in your ride and get the hell out of there before anyone notices your foul handiwork.

Or, if you're like us and love a good laugh, put a box labeled "FREE BEER & DONUTS" under the seat to catch your droppings, then close it up, and leave it where it's sure to be discovered and opened.

75

MR. T AIR FRESHENER

LOCATION: Boca Raton, FL

COST: $6.99

DESCRIPTION:

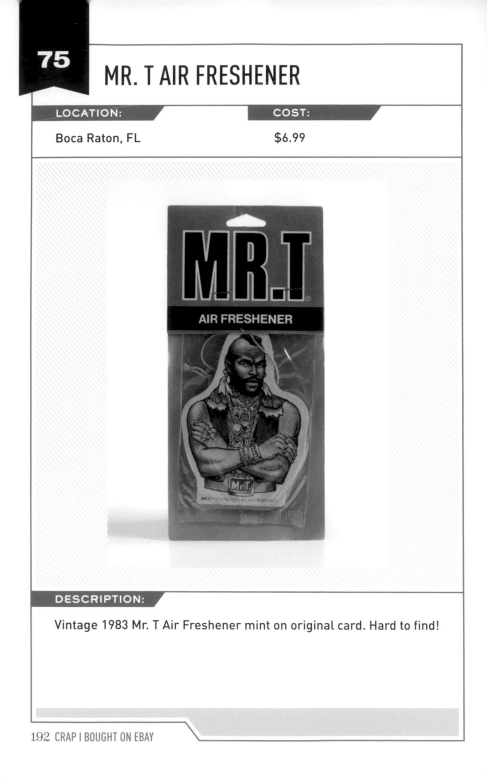

Vintage 1983 Mr. T Air Freshener mint on original card. Hard to find!

Have you ever said to yourself, "I sure wish my car smelled like that big sweaty black guy from *The A-Team*"? We have, and that's why we grabbed the Mr. T Air Freshener the second we saw it listed on eBay.

We won't lie: we love Mr. T. *LOVE*. The mohawk, the bling, the speech impediment, all of it. Say what you will about the man—he is original.

When Mr T. hit the scene in 1982, he immediately became a huge star, probably because no one had ever seen a grown man dress like he did who wasn't 1) mentally handicapped or 2) a member of the Village People. He got a hit TV series and a Saturday morning cartoon. He made records, videos, and books for kids. They put his face and name on every crappy product they could find, from breakfast cereal to soap on a rope to this, of all things, an air freshener. And that's how you know you've arrived: they put your face on a deodorizing product.

We hung the Mr. T Air Freshener from the rearview mirror in our Plymouth Volare, and it really makes a statement. That statement is this: "I pity the fool who tries to smoke or eat chicken wings in this car, because I will beat you like a sucka!" Look at the man's face; he's serious about freshness.

If you're wondering what the Mr. T Air Freshener smells like, it smells like an ass-whupping, that's what. So don't even think about stinking up our car, fool.

76

"I LOVE MY CLITORIS!" REVENGE BUMPER STICKER

LOCATION:

Hell, USA

COST:

$3.99

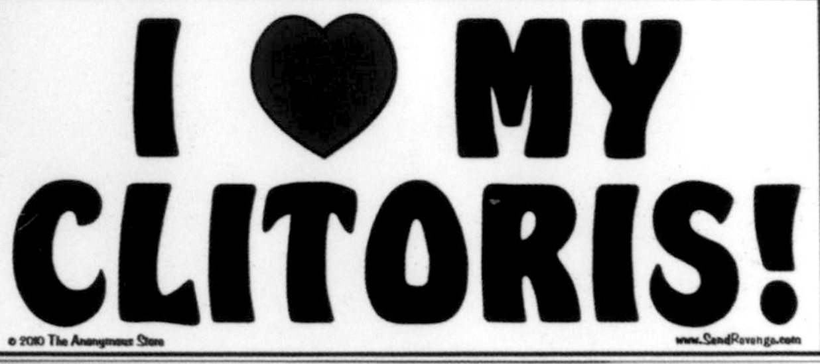

DESCRIPTION:

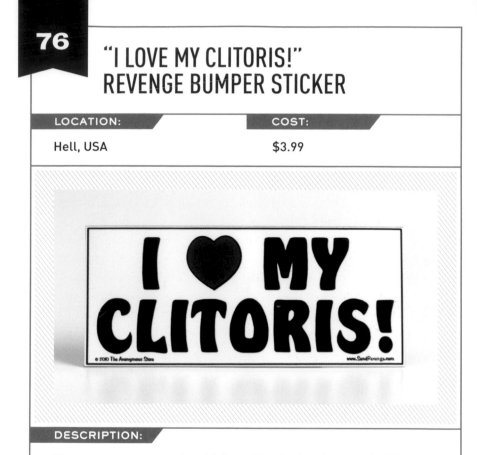

Place one on someone's vehicle and let the laughter begin! Play a joke on your Homophobic or Overly Macho Friend! Also great for Ex-Boyfriends/Girlfriends, Brothers/Sisters, Bosses, Co-Workers, Teachers, Neighbors, or for Anyone you want to PRANK! GOOD CLEAN FUN!

Who doesn't love the clitoris? It's a tiny ball of nerves that, when stimulated properly, sends women into toe-curling, ecstatic orbit. That is, if you can find it, which some men couldn't do even with spelunking gear, a map, and a flashlight.

No matter how much we adore our love button (and we do), we'd never willingly announce to the world that we rub 'em out on the regular, which is why putting this sticker on someone's car is the perfect way to exact revenge and let them know that they fucked with the wrong person. We usually throw a brick through their windshield or key their car, but this is a little more subtle and less likely to land you in the slammer.

Pranks are fun, but we don't think we know anyone we dislike so intensely that we'd actually stick a revenge bumper sticker on their car. Well, maybe that's not entirely true; we do have a healthy dislike for some of our a-hole coworkers. The next time one of them complains that we're out of coffee creamer, we may just give them something else to complain about, like being rear-ended by motorists who are too busy laughing at their incredibly out-there bumper sticker to notice that they've stopped at a red light.

Speaking of out-there, we've got some more suggestions for the revenge sticker industry. Here are some we'd like to see printed up:

Ask me about
MY CLITORIS!

My clitoris was
Clitoris of the Month!

My clitoris beat up
your honor student.
I'D RATHER BE PLAYING
WITH MY CLITORIS.
If you can read this,
you're too close
to my clitoris!

We think we've got a future here. If this whole eBay book-writing thing doesn't work out for us, we're heading into the world of revenge bumper stickers.

77

FURRY BOOBS

LOCATION:

Manchester, UK

COST:

GBP 5.99 ($9.27 US)

DESCRIPTION:

BRAND NEW, ADULTS ONLY. FURRY BOOBS. STROKE YOUR ROAD RAGE AWAY WITH THESE FURRY BOOBS. YOUR NAUGHTY VEHICLE ACCESSORY!!! BEATS THE FURRY DICE ANYDAY!!!

When you think of a woman's breasts, "furry" is not really the image you want to see in your mind's eye. Sure, some gals will sprout the occasional wild hair in their areolae, but those can be plucked, preferably before a husband or boyfriend spots it in bed and suddenly decides he's not interested in playing Hide the Salami after all.

"Furry boobs" conjures up visions of mammaries completely covered in hair, the kind you may find on Madonna, Dr. Zira in *Planet of the Apes*, or Sasquatch's wife, Marjory Finnegan-Sasquatch.

We were relieved, then, to see that these furry boobs are merely a perverted spin on the old furry dice that hipsters once hung from their rearview mirrors to be hip, and post-ironic hipsters still hang from theirs to be hip, but with a much higher rate of failure to achieve hipness.

They are also a great illustration of the fundamental differences between men and women. Many men who see these on eBay will chuckle and think, "Those are hilarious. I should get some for my car." Not that they will, but they are at least willing to entertain the idea.

If the product was a furry cock-and-balls set instead, how many women do you think would 1) laugh at it, and 2) even consider buying it? We're guessing five and zero, respectively, for the entire world. The same goes for furry boobs or any other sexual organ turned into a plush toy: not really a good way to get action.

So, men, you have a decision: be the funny immature guy with furry boobs in his ride to amuse his friends, or the guy who's smart enough not to put furry boobs in his car because he wants to continue seeing the real things on a regular basis. Your choice.

78

CORN DOG AIR FRESHENERS

LOCATION:

Chula Vista, CA

COST:

$3.95

DESCRIPTION:

The corn dog is quite possibly the best food on a stick ever created! Close your eyes and you can almost smell the sweet honey batter and the steaming, salty meat product nestled inside. This 6¼" long air freshener has the sharp aroma of bright yellow mustard, which might not make your car smell the best, but it will make all of your passengers drool. Comes with a string for hanging.

Wait, since when would we *purposely make* our car smell like mustard? We're not talking about fresh-baked cookies here, or even Cheerios, we're talking about mustard, the same stuff that once rendered Bev's minivan a chamber of olfactory horrors until she was forced to excavate the entire back half of the vehicle to find the half-eaten corn dog that her slovenly child had so thoughtlessly dropped and failed to mention to her. Fucking kids!

And who would want a corn dog dangling from their rearview mirror in the first place? Does anyone love corn dogs that much? We can't think of anyone. Carnies, maybe, but we don't know any of those, thank God.

We suppose if you drive one of those trucks that looks like a giant hot dog in a bun, it may make sense to have the cab smell like mustard. After all, you've obviously already given up your dignity once you agreed to man the wiener wagon, so what's one more detail to complete the image? But if you drive a regular car, there's really no excuse to drape a cardboard corn dog around your mirror and treat your passengers to the lingering scent of mustard.

If you like mustard we could develop a whole slew of bizarre scents. Who says air fresheners have to smell *fresh*? Screw pine trees; they're passé. We'd like to see a taco air freshener, or maybe something musky like sweat sock or day-old coitus. Why limit yourself? Life is short.

79

"ASS: THE OTHER VAGINA" STICKER

LOCATION:

Daytona Beach, FL

COST:

$2.75

DESCRIPTION:

Durable UV resistant weatherproof high quality easy peel and stick-on vinyl sticker. 1½" × 3" (3.75 cm × 7.50 cm). Will not crack or fade. Will not damage surface, easy to remove. Perfect for your car, truck, van, SUV, station wagon, hot rod, street rod, lowrider, pickup, motorcycle, skateboard, surfboard, boat, airplane, train, etc. The sky is the limit.

Okay, we'll admit it, this sticker made us laugh. We never thought of the ass in those exact terms, but now that you mention it, okay. You could have a sticker that says, "I (heart) anal sex" or "Stick it in my pooper," but it just wouldn't have the same pop as this one.

Still, you wonder who would put this on his car, truck, SUV, station wagon, hot rod, street rod, etc. We say *his* because no self-respecting woman would tell the world that she takes it up the back stairway—and not just every now and then, but so often that her husband thinks of her anus as a second vagina. Nothing against butt sex, but just because something is true doesn't mean you have to tell everyone about it.

If we saw this sticker on the freeway, we would have to speed up alongside the vehicle to see what kind of freak would display such a thing. In this case, it would probably be a pickup truck or a Harley, with a man driving and a woman in the passenger seat, no doubt sitting on one of those rubber donut cushions they give to people with hemorrhoids. We would stare and laugh and point and honk until the female passenger hid her face in shame. When the guy looked at us, we would give him a big thumbs-up and mouth the words, "FUCK YEAH!" while we made the classic "banging the Mrs. up the butt" gesture.

Then, since we weren't paying attention to the road, we'd slam into a bridge abutment and die instantly, which would serve us right for making fun of people for their sexual habits, however deviant they may be.

ARE YOU GONNA EAT THAT CRAP?

FUNKED-UP FOOD

When we look at food, we see dinner. When some people look at food, they see pixies or the Virgin Mary or Mickey Rooney's nutsack. And then they see dollars. Good for them for having a vivid imagination; we're always too hungry to study our food for signs from above (or below).

Prepare yourself for a handful of WTF? food items that should be in a pot of soup, not on eBay. Except we bought them, so look for more in the future. Why do we encourage these people?

80

SCREAMING SPHINCTER CAYENNE HOT SAUCE

LOCATION:

Charlotte, NC

COST:

$6.50

DESCRIPTION:

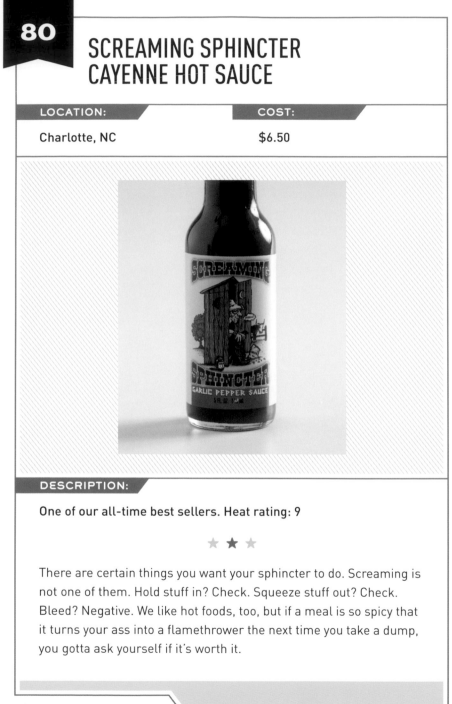

One of our all-time best sellers. Heat rating: 9

There are certain things you want your sphincter to do. Screaming is not one of them. Hold stuff in? Check. Squeeze stuff out? Check. Bleed? Negative. We like hot foods, too, but if a meal is so spicy that it turns your ass into a flamethrower the next time you take a dump, you gotta ask yourself if it's worth it.

Anyone who's had inferno-style hot wings knows that the real test of your mettle comes not when you eat them, but the next day, when you release them back into the wild.

"WTF," you say to yourself, "I don't remember eating the *SUN*."

After you've jammed a couple of ice cubes up your hole to ease the pain, you have to check the bowl extra careful-like to make sure there's no blood or bits of tissue in there, which for us was the clincher (pun intended). We would much rather go without eating nuclear hot wings forever than have to inspect our turds that closely again.

But the world is full of sadists who enjoy having a charred butt-hole, and products like this are made for them. Screaming Sphincter Hot Sauce is advertised as "a burning painus in the anus," which is sort of cute, but we think we can do better. Here are some alternate taglines for the product that we hope the manufacturer might consider:

DON'T IT MAKE YOUR BROWN EYE BLUE (AND BLACK)?

PUT A ZING IN YOUR O-RING!

FIRE IN THE HOLE!

It'll wreck your rectum.

Shit Fire!

You'll need salve for that swollen valve.

81

DEER JERKY SHAPED LIKE USA

LOCATION:

USA

COST:

$2

DESCRIPTION:

THIS IS A UNIQUE ITEM. THIS DEER JERKEY WAS PULLED OUT OF THE BAG LOOKING VERY, VERY SIMILAR TO A MAP OF THE US. IT WOULD MAKE A GREAT HOLIDAY GIFT FOR THE PERSON WHO IS IMPOSSIBLE TO BUY FOR. BATTERY NOT INCLUDED, IN PHOTO FOR SIZE COMPARISON ONLY. NOT FOR CONSUMPTION. ENTERTAINMENT VALUE ONLY.

Mm, deer jerky. Salty, gamey, *and* chewy? Our cup runneth over. Oh, but you can't actually eat this piece—sorry! We love how the seller listed all those caveats in the description: don't eat it, it's for entertainment purposes only, that battery is *not* included so don't even think you're getting your mitts on it. What a way to take all the fun out of a tiny chunk of dead deer carcass.

Claiming that this tidbit of dried venison looks like the United States is a bit of a stretch. After all, it's missing one very important component: America's wang! What has become of the great state of Florida? And have we taken over a portion of Mexico? Damn it, these questions demanded answers, so of course we asked the seller.

↗ Dear JerkStore,

Cool item. Did someone eat Florida?

S. Finkter

↗ Dear S. Finkter,

Ha, no. It doesn't have anything missing, this is how it came out of the bag.

JerkStore

↗ Dear JerkStore,

Can you throw in the battery? I need one for my vibrator.

S. Finkter

↗ Dear S. Finkter,

Sorry, the battery is just to show scale and size. It is not included.

JerkStore

↗ Dear JerkStore,

Deal breaker. I really wanted that battery. Let me know if you change your mind.

S. Finkter

Nah, we bought it anyway, of course, but when we got this item in the mail, the first thing we realized was that the seller was totally right: it tasted terrible. We could barely choke it down, but hey, there isn't much we wouldn't do for this book. You can thank us later.

82

ONE OF A KIND CARROT

LOCATION: Massachusetts, USA

COST: $0.99

DESCRIPTION:

A one of a kind item up for auction! Not just any carrot, but an organic carrot! I don't really know what could of caused this carrot to turn out so odd, looking like it has legs and questionable genitalia . . . but for those of you who like to collect unusual things, this could be a great addition to your collection.

This, we're told, is an organic carrot, which in this case, means that it appears to have an organ, and of the male sexual variety. We think. That bump could be something that needs to be lanced, like a boil or the world's largest genital wart. It also has the worst case of eczema we've ever seen; either that, or it spent the last year in someone's colon.

This strange little vegetable arrived at our door in bad shape: cold, dirty, mute, and completely inedible. We immediately gave him a hot bath and a good peeling, and only after layers of dirt were removed did we realize something incredible: this carrot is not a he, but a she. That's not the world's smallest penis; it's the world's biggest clitoris. Step aside, Joanie "Chyna" Laurer.

Unfortunately, it's also about three inches west of where it should be, and in a position on the front of the leg where it is subject to constant stimulation, as opposed to the traditional placement of the clitoris in a top-secret location that's nearly impossible for most men to find, but free from all but the most intentional agitation.

We tried to remedy the situation by taping a quarter on one side of the organ to promote growth back toward the crotch. But, the carrot, whom we named Eileen because of her mismatched legs, was not exactly compliant. In fact, she removed every quarter we taped to her until it became clear that she did not want her clitoris moved to a place of less stimulation.

Eileen continues to recuperate, but soon she and her ginormous mutant clit will be ready to re-enter society. When they do, they are going to make some guy carrot very happy.

83

LEMON SHAPED LIKE HEAD STICKING OUT TONGUE

LOCATION:	COST:
Los Angeles, CA	$2.99

DESCRIPTION:

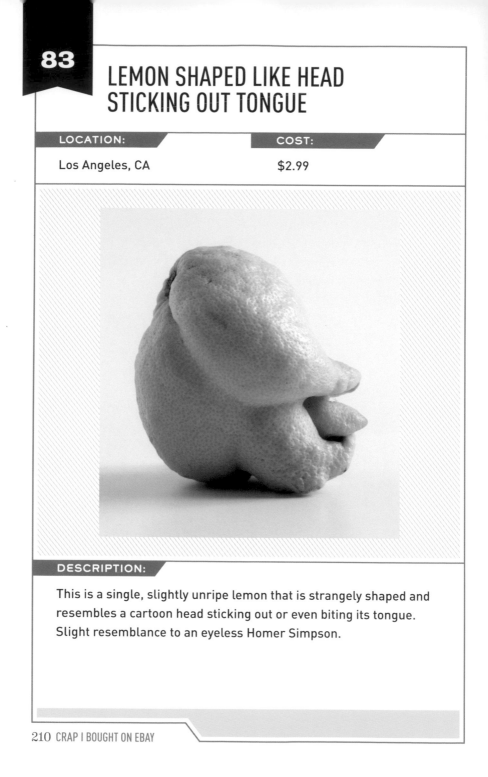

This is a single, slightly unripe lemon that is strangely shaped and resembles a cartoon head sticking out or even biting its tongue. Slight resemblance to an eyeless Homer Simpson.

What's that expression? "When life hands you deformed lemons, sell them on eBay?" Something like that.

When we first saw this lemon, we were tilting our heads and scratching our chins, squinting at it and saying, "Hmmm," and "Hrrrmmm," until we finally saw what the seller was seeing. It still mostly looks like a funked-up lemon to us, but we suppose we can go along with the whole "cannibalistic lemon eating another lemon" thing.

If we squint hard enough, now that ya mention it, yes! It does look a tiny bit like Homer Simpson—throwing up.

Why anyone would want to *own* a lemon that looks like a yacking Homer Simpson is beyond us, so we asked the seller.

↗ Dear Sourpuss,

Why are you selling a lemon on eBay?

S. Finkter

↗ Dear S. Finkter,

We just thought this one was cool because it's shaped like a head eating something. Thanks for looking!

Sourpuss

↗ Dear Sourpuss,

Do you get mutant lemons often? What causes the mutations?

Sourpuss

↗ Dear S. Finkter,

Yeah, but this is the first one we've listed. Sometimes they just come funny.

Sourpuss

↗ Dear Sourpuss,

That's what she said. But how will it taste? (Also what she said.)

S. Finkter

↗ Dear S. Finkter,

Like a lemon.

Sourpuss

Something tells us that Sourpuss was tired of hearing from us, so we went ahead and bought his darn malformed lemon. It was the least we could do for a fellow *Simpsons* fan.

84

ODD POTATO SHAPED LIKE FROG

LOCATION: Waterloo, IA

COST: $0.59

DESCRIPTION:

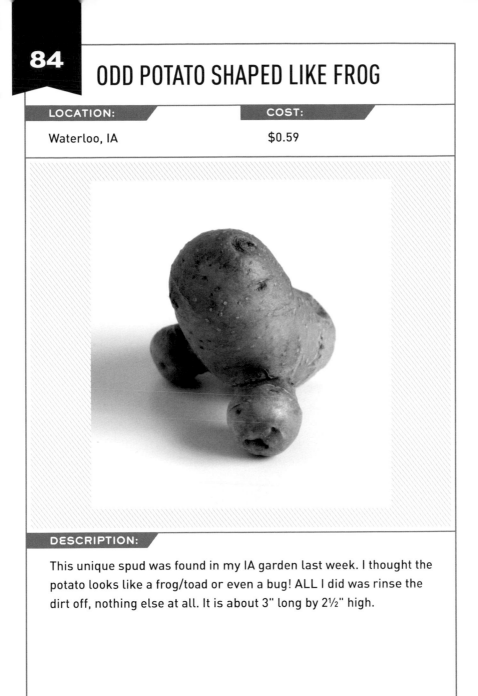

This unique spud was found in my IA garden last week. I thought the potato looks like a frog/toad or even a bug! ALL I did was rinse the dirt off, nothing else at all. It is about 3" long by 2½" high.

Hey, look at this effed-up-looking potato. It looks like Kermit the Frog and Miss Piggy finally produced a mutant love child with no eyes and only two legs, which is pretty much what we suspect would happen if a frog really knocked up a pig.

We honestly didn't know what to make of this item. It's even less impressive-looking in person, so it's hard to imagine that some Iowa gardener pulled this spud out of the earth and said, "Hurrah! This potato verily resembles a frog. Perhaps I shall list it on eBay and fetch a fanciful price!" (That's how we imagine people talk in Iowa.)

Yet someone did just that, and here we sit looking at a green potato that *vaguely* resembles a rather hoity-toity amphibian. In related news, did you know that there is an *Urban Dictionary* definition for "potato frog"? It makes absolutely no sense, but here it is:

> Potato frog: A type of frog that tastes like potatoes. It likes the taste of paper. There is only one potato frog in the world, because THERE CAN ONLY BE ONE. If at any time there were two potato frogs, then the first one would go all granny on its butt.

WTF? Whoever wrote that entry was on some serious drugs. Maybe the author licked a toxic toad and came up with that definition whilst traipsing through a magical forest filled with unicorns and pixie dust.

We wrote the seller to ask for a few suggestions on how to best utilize this unique piece of crap, but she never responded. Maybe it was the part of our email when we asked, "Will this fit up my ass?" that turned her off; we can't be sure. All we know is that we now have a rapidly decaying potato in our possession and not the faintest idea of what to do with it.

We finally decided to fry it up and eat it. Oddly enough, it tasted like chicken.

HAVE YOURSELF A CRAPPY LITTLE CHRISTMAS

MAKE THE YULETIDE LAME

You don't have to search on eBay for long to find lots of crazy holiday decorations for revelers with highly questionable taste. Some people really go all out when decorating for the holidays, after all. If your idea of festive décor involves sitting on Santa's face, displaying a blasphemous Nativity scene in your bathroom, or freaking out your kids with a creepy clown doll, this is your one-stop shop. These items are guaranteed to land you at the top of Santa's naughty list—and a seat in Hell.

85

RUBBER DUCKIE CHRISTMAS NATIVITY SCENE

LOCATION:

Georgia, USA

COST:

$5.85

DESCRIPTION:

What a clever way to display the nativity scene! Each ducky measures approx. 2" × 2" with the lamb and baby Jesus measuring a little bit smaller, approx 1.5" × 1.5". They don't squeak, but they do have a tiny hole in the beak so they can squirt water in the tub. They do not float upright. Great for party favors at church functions, bible studies, or Sunday school prizes.

FADE IN

HEAVEN—GOD'S CABANA—LATE AFTERNOON

GOD sits on a ginormous solid gold throne by the beach, reading a document with His feet up, sipping a frosty beverage. We hear harp music and much mirth. In the background, a group of beautiful topless women giggle and play with a beach ball. Handsome young bohunks give massages to exhausted moms at the water's edge. A five-story keg dispenses imported beer to all revelers while Joan of Arc grills fat juicy steaks and corn on the cob for everyone.

CLOSE-UP SHOT of document. The header reads: "Daily Blasphemy Report."

GOD

(reading and muttering to Himself)

Marilyn Manson: has-been, nobody cares. Madonna: ditto. South Park: old news. Rubber duck Nativ—RUBBER DUCK NATIVITY?!!!"

We hear a collective GASP as everyone freezes. The harp music stops with a sour note. The beach ball hits a topless woman in the head. A huge ribeye steak falls to the sand.

GOD hurls the document to the ground, then grabs a phone.

GOD

(into phone)

My cabana! NOW! And bring the Smiting Machine.

We've seen some questionable Nativity scenes in our day, everything from dogs to aliens, to the Three Stooges as the Magi, but this one may take the booby prize. Rubber duckies are cute, sure, but we're not getting the whole Holy-Family-as-waterfowl motif.

We picture the Nativity as a quiet, reverential moment, not a midnight clear filled with the incessant quack-quack-quacking of ducks. Could they have picked a noisier animal? Maybe they'll make a geese Nativity scene next. And then donkeys. Or elephants.

CUT TO:

EARTH—SOMEONE'S BATHROOM—MORNING

STEVE, creator of the Rubber Duck Nativity set, plays with his new toys in a bubble bath and is delighted with himself.

STEVE

These are so AWESO—

A sudden LIGHTNING BOLT turns Steve into a suspended heap of ash with eyes, like a cartoon. The eyes blink in shock.

STEVE

Ouch.

Steve's ashes fall to the water.

FADE OUT

86

FATHER CHRISTMAS TOILET SEAT COVER

LOCATION:

Essex, UK

COST:

$3.18 (US)

DESCRIPTION:

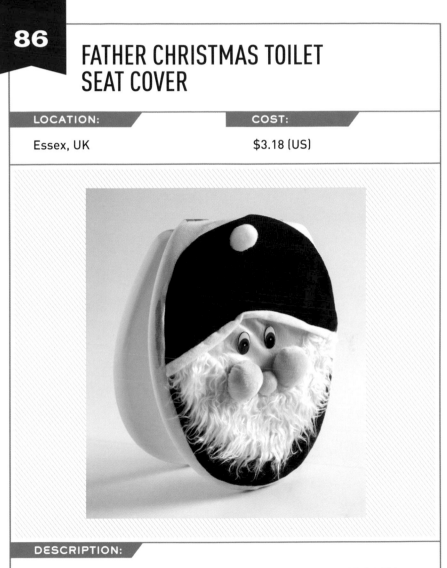

BRAND NEW NOVELTY DECORATION FOR THE SMALLEST ROOM IN YOUR HOUSE. SIMPLY STRETCHES OVER THE LID OF YOUR TOILET TO BRING A TOUCH OF FESTIVE CHEER. SHOULD FIT MOST TOILETS, BUT THEY NEED TO BE STRETCHED QUITE TIGHT.

"You better watch out, you better not cry, you better not pout I'm tellin' you why, Santa Claus is watching . . . you poop." Oh, come on, haven't you always wanted to sit on Santa's face? What could be more festive than having a cheerful St. Nick face made of fabric (which doesn't act as a germ sponge at all, we're sure) staring at you when you enter the commode to do your bidness? Not much, we say. Not much at all. We had just a few questions for the seller, naturally.

↗ Dear Saint Dick,

Is this toilet seat cover supposed to be terrifying? Thanks.

S. Finkter

What? We're just being honest.

↗ Dear S. Finkter,

No, it's meant to be cheerful. It's a Christmas decoration.

Saint Dick

We think it missed the mark.

↗ Dear Saint Dick,

Okay. Is it washable? Won't it get covered in fecal germs?

S. Finkter

↗ Dear S. Finkter,

It is not machine-washable but you can hand-wash it.

Saint Dick

Yeah, that's gonna happen!

For what it's worth, the jolly Santa face was only mildly unnerving when we placed it on our crapper. It's kind of like Santa is hungry for our poo, which is a good thing, because he'll get plenty in there.

87

MUSICAL CLOWN SANTA

LOCATION:

California, USA

COST:

$35

DESCRIPTION:

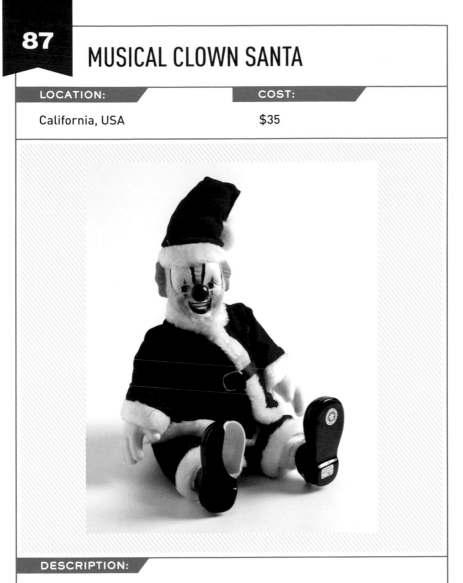

Musical Clown porcelain Santa. Very good condition, like new, have the original box. Plays a few different parts of Christmas songs. Purchased in the late '80s. Made by Victoria Impex Corp. This was an expensive item, over $75.00.

Remember when all you had to do to keep kids in line during the holidays was remind them that Santa Claus was watching their behavior, shaking his head, and making little frowny faces next to their names on his list? Those days are long gone.

Kids today are too savvy. They know that no matter what you threaten, Santa always brings them a good haul on Christmas morning. They don't know the real reason for this—that you're competing with all your friends to see who looks like they have the most money. They only know there's no way they'll get just a lump of coal from Santa, probably because they don't even know what coal is.

That's why we're thrilled to introduce to you Mr. Musical Clown Santa. This creepy motherfucker is guaranteed to give your wee ones a Christmas they'll never forget. Clowns are scary enough on their own, but give them a Santa hat and a demented "I'm going to eat you" smile, and you've got one kid-motivating sonofabitch to use however you see fit. Who needs an elf on the shelf when you've got the Devil in your den?

If your incorrigible child isn't troubled by the thought of fewer toys on Christmas morn, let him wake in the middle of the night with this demon sitting at the foot of his bed, glaring him down and playing creepy Christmas music that sounds like Hell's ice cream truck. He will magically transform into a little angel, and stay that way at least until June, when you can bring out the Beast again as a reminder that he's being watched not just at Christmas, but year-round.

"On the first day of Christmas, my parents gave to me, a scary doll that wants to eat my face."

88

KENNY ROGERS GLASS BALL LIMITED EDITION ORNAMENT

LOCATION:

Ithaca, NY

COST:

$0.99

DESCRIPTION:

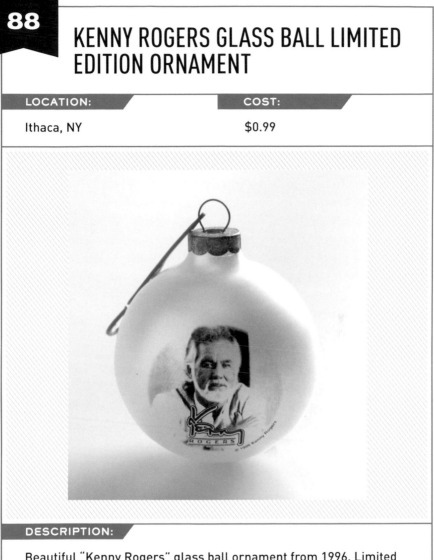

Beautiful "Kenny Rogers" glass ball ornament from 1996. Limited edition ornament is a fabulous find for that country rock lover. Don't miss your chance to own this rare collectible at this low price!

A Kenny Rogers limited edition Christmas tree ornament for ninety-nine cents? What, are you nuts?! This thing is worth at least ten times what he's asking; it's like finding a Mickey Mantle rookie baseball card at a yard sale for a nickel.

If you know anything at all about Christmas tree ornaments, you know that the '96 Kenny is considered a Holy Grail of ornament collecting for several reasons. It was the only premium ever given out with the two-piece gizzard snack at Kenny Rogers' Roasters restaurant before that menu item was discontinued a year later. The glass in the ornament was lovingly blown by master artisans from the finest Arabian sand. Kenny's signature on the ball is a certified authentic facsimile of his actual hand-penned signature. Perhaps most importantly of all, the ball features the likeness of pre-plastic surgery Kenny, before he became someone else.

We're still pinching ourselves to be sure we actually bought this thing for under a buck. Most of you don't know it, but we have one of the largest Kenny Rogers memorabilia collections in the world, which already includes several Kenny velvet paintings, one of which actually sort of resembles him; a rare frame of videotape from the classic film, *Kenny Rogers as the Gambler, Part III: The Legend Continues*; a cocktail napkin from Caesar's Palace in Las Vegas, signed by Kenny's cousin's husband, Lamar; and a thimble full of clippings from Kenny's beard.

Add to that list the 1996 Kenny Rogers Glass Ball Limited Edition Ornament. Then color us giddy.

89

CHRISTMAS BOUNCING BELLS/ BOOBS CAN COOZIE

LOCATION:	COST:
USA	$8.99

DESCRIPTION:

Bobble Babes Christmas Can Cooler everyone will have fun with this one. The Boobs are made with bells instead of silicone. Get yours early limited supplies.

We know that during the holiday season people tend to ride the Crazy Horse more often, and we're here to help. What can we say? We're givers. With that in mind, we bring you the perfect gift for the beer-swilling crap-lover in your life: a jingle boobs beer coozie! That's right: it's a floozy on a coozie, and that beer must be really cold because her nipples are hard enough to poke your eye out, kid.

If your idea of spreading Christmas cheer is enjoying a nice Boobweiser or Tits, er, Schlitz, why not jazz up the boring old can with this cool item? It's functional *and* festive, and you can't deny that whoever uses it is a connoisseur of classy conversation pieces.

This beer coozie may just be the perfect way to jazz up your Christmas caroling routine. Pour yourself a mug of your poison of choice (in our case, Bourbon with a splash of eggnog), slip the Bouncing Boobs Beer Coozie into your mug, and prepare for the hilarity to ensue! Your neighbors, who are no doubt used to you classing up the joint, will be delighted by the melodious jingling sound that will accompany you getting absolutely shit-faced while you butcher the words to "Good King Wenceslas."

Maybe we're wrong here, of course. It's entirely possible that we're being overly harsh or elitist toward the sort of folks who would utilize a beer coozie with a pair of jiggling, bouncing bell boobs on it. Perhaps monocle-wearing, brandy-sipping multimillionaires also find these jingle boobs hilarious—but we doubt it.

90

1946 TURKEY WISHBONE

LOCATION: Springfield, OR

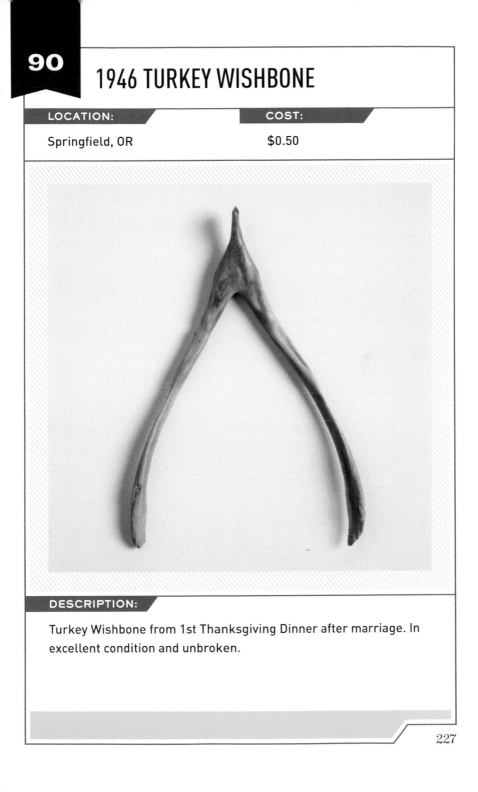

COST: $0.50

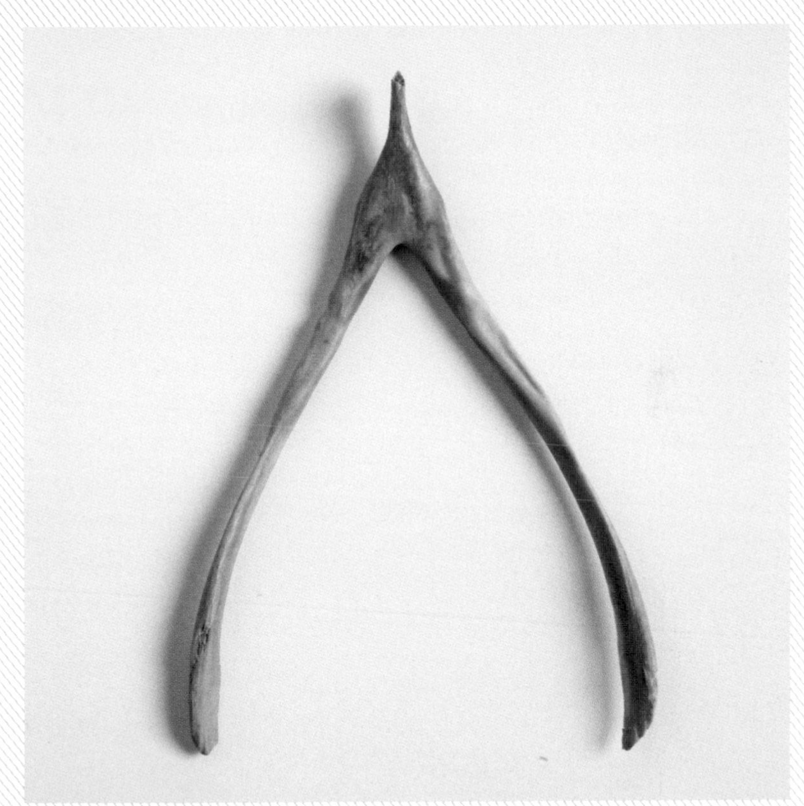

DESCRIPTION:

Turkey Wishbone from 1st Thanksgiving Dinner after marriage. In excellent condition and unbroken.

Where else but eBay would you find a sixty-four-year-old wishbone? People save the strangest things.

When Cary was in college, he and a few other students helped a professor and his family move. While the boys loaded up furniture, the professor's wife cleaned out the freezer. She pulled out a bag of what looked like frozen chicken broth with a baby octopus in it, then excitedly said to her husband, "Oh, look, Matty's placenta. We forgot to plant it." Huh? The professor explained that wherever he was from (Arkansas? Neptune?), it is considered good luck to save a baby's placenta and plant it with a tree in your yard. Cary considered it good luck that he had never eaten anything out of these people's freezer. So it could be worse—this bone could be placenta goo. The note on the bone reads:

> Turkey wishbone. From 1st Thanksgiving Dinner after Hayes and I were married, April 17, 1946. —Millie

Kind of sweet, isn't it? Weird and creepy, but sweet. One can only assume that Hayes and Millie are no longer with us (in body and/or mind), but this strange yet touching keepsake of their years together remains.

On eBay.

For fifty cents.

CRAP WE WANTED TO BUY BUT COULDN'T

WHAT ARE WE, MADE OF MONEY?

Just because we're big successful writers doesn't mean we're loaded with cash. Besides, even rich people see things they want but aren't willing to fork over the asking price.

Yes, of course we'd love to own our own tank, but an extra 350 Gs is tough to come by in this economy. As much as we would love to give some stranger's kid-to-be a stupid name like Mike Rotch or Wilma Fingerdoo, it's not worth $40,000 to us, especially when we'll never be able to laugh at him in person. Ditto for items like a crystal rat coffin or a severed head or our own airport tower. Cool stuff, and we're happy to write about it, but there's no way in hell we're buying it.

Unless, of course, you'd like to donate to our cause.

91

PROSTHETIC LEG BUCCANEERS NFL

LOCATION:

New Port Richey, FL

COST:

$649.99

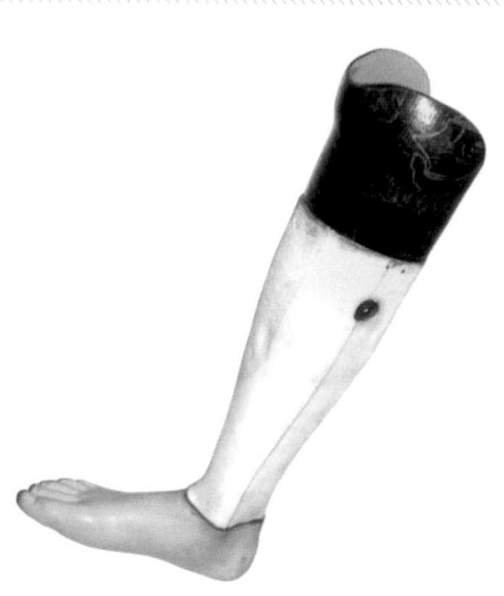

DESCRIPTION:

PROSTHETIC right LEG (20¼" tall). No Markings . . . foot measures 9" long × 3" widest. Big toe hanging, and another toe nail missing. SOLD AS IS No Returns.

If you're like us and have a running list of Things That Would Totally Suck, add this to it: losing a leg. For starters, it probably hurts like hell when you lose it. It's also totally embarrassing to be short one appendage; people stare and children point. Then you have to go out and find a replacement leg, which costs an arm and—uh, a lot of money. So you go on eBay to look for a gently used leg at a good price, and instead, you see crap like this thing with a Tampa Bay Buccaneers football team logo on it. Har har, a pirate's peg-leg, very funny, motherfucker. We don't need the leg, but we wanted to berate the seller for his insensitivity.

↗ Dear Capt. Schnook,

Nice leg, but what's with the Tampa Bay Bucs theme? Did it belong to a Bucs player? Or is this your idea of a bad pirate joke? Because I'm not laughing.

S. Finkter

He actually replied.

↗ Dear S. Finkter,

I don't get the Bucs either, sorry. I bought it at an estate sale.

Capt. Schnook

Ah, so the owner died and now his children are selling off everything he owned, and we do mean everything. "How much do you think we can get for Dad's leg?"

↗ Dear Capt. Schnook,

Fine. What kind of wear and tear are we talking here? Light home/office use, or was the guy like a soccer player or grape stomper or something?

S. Finkter

Another reply. He must really want to sell this thing.

↗ Dear S. Finkter,

The wear and tear is from casual office/home/light leisure use. Not used in rigorous activities, although 10 years of on and off use does take its toll.

Capt. Schnook

Fair enough. One final rattle on his cage:

↗ Dear Capt. Schnook,

Great. I'll take it. Do you offer next-day shipping? I need the leg for an ass-kicking contest this weekend.

S. Finkter

No reply. Fine, we don't have the $650, anyway.

92

GIANT TYRANNOSAURUS REX LIFE-SIZE STATUE JURASSIC PARK

LOCATION:

Hilton Head, SC

COST:

$27,500 plus $4,500 S/H

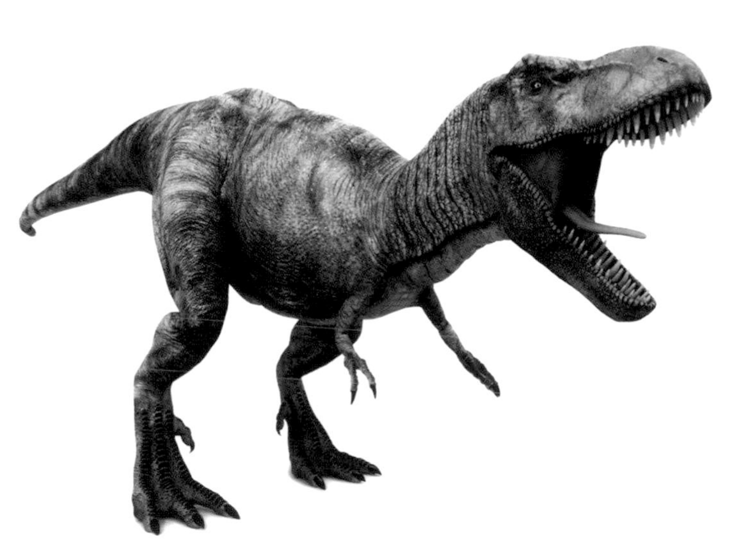

DESCRIPTION:

Giant Lifesize T Rex Statue stands over 20 Foot Tall. Most of our large dinosaurs require a crane to assemble. Don't miss all our other dinosaur statues and theme park or amusement park size items.

If we ever win the lottery and have money coming out of our ears, we'd totally get eccentric and start collecting random useless (but undeniably cool) pieces of crap like this one. Seriously, who *doesn't* want a life-sized T-Rex?

Look at this thing. Look at it! It's *fabulous*. If we had an extra thirty-two grand on us, we would SO buy this puppy and put it right in the front yard. In the summer, we'd put a giant bikini on it. In the winter, we'd throw on a Santa hat during the holidays. Maybe some cheery flowers in his tiny T-Rex arms during the spring, and you've got yourself the coolest lawn ornament ever! Rex would be the crown jewel of any neighborhood. We know our neighbors would love it.

This life-sized T-Rex was probably made for museums, movies, and the like, but how cool is it that you can buy one on eBay? Aside from making your garden gnomes and gazing balls look pathetic by comparison, we wondered what else we could do with it. Here's what we came up with:

1. Hollow out the inside and make it into a Trojan T-Rex; win battles by sheer cunning.
2. Hmmm . . . coming up with uses for this thing was way harder than we thought it would be. Maybe it's okay that we can't afford it after all.

93

AIRPORT CONTROL TOWER

LOCATION:

Three Rivers, MI

COST:

$12,500

DESCRIPTION:

Do you have problems when giving directions to your location and people just can't seem to find your house? Put this up and it will greatly aid in people finding you. Or if you are an aviation buff, how about putting this up next to your hangar at the airport. This is an actual airport control tower made of structural grade ¼" aluminum and can be dissambled fairly easily. It has three (3) levels. There is a small trap door to access the cat walk, a custom built angled sofa, the walls are tongue and groove cedar, the glass is all good with no cracks or discolorations. I will even throw in a bunch of rope lights I used to decorate it for Christmas.

We think it's wonderful to live in a country where you can buy *entire buildings* on an online auction site. Who knew? That reminds us—we have a cathedral we need to unload. It's big, but don't worry, it "dissambles" pretty easily. The shipping may be a bit high, but we'll try to keep it under $70,000.

Just kidding, we love this tower—what a simple and elegant solution to a difficult-to-find address. Who needs MapQuest? Just erect this beacon in your yard; they'll find you. Who cares about zoning ordinances, pissed-off neighbors, or planes crash-landing into your house because they think you're an airport?

Cary really wants this thing, and he's already called dibs on it if he can ever put his hands on a spare $12,500. He has a daughter approaching teendom, you see, and it's only a matter of time before the boys come sniffing around and try to sneak into her window late at night. Imagine their surprise when the spotlight hits them, the alarm horns start blaring, and Cary mows them down with the .50 caliber machine gun he mounted on the tower. "And *stay* out!"

94

USMC M60A1 TANK

LOCATION:

Texas, USA

COST:

$350,000

DESCRIPTION:

Original Desert Storm veteran USMC M60A1 Main battle tank. With rare late production inert reactive armor package. One of the few in civilian hands. Original Continental 12 cyl. twin turbocharged air cooled diesel engine is in perfect running condition with all new road wheels and like new track. Includes replica 105MM shells in all of the racks.

Isn't it funny how sometimes you don't realize you need something until you see it? A back scratcher, for example, or that upside-down tomato planter. Or a tank. That's right: a real, honest-to-goodness, armor-reinforced, fire-breathing, ordnance-hurling, Commie-killing, battlefield behemoth. Who knew you could buy war machines on eBay? Sweet Jesus, we love the Internet.

Take a moment to imagine the things you could do with this little problem-solver. Close your eyes and savor the utterly delicious possibilities of driving a sixty-ton, solid-steel all-terrain vehicle with two machine guns and a cannon that fires shells bigger than your arm. We did, and we saw a world without tailgaters, horn-honkers, lane-blockers, brake-riders, zig-zaggers, cell phone users, and "Turn signal? What's that?"-ers.

We had some questions for the seller, whom we pictured as a no-nonsense military man, the kind of lifelong jarhead who still gets up before daybreak to do chin-ups and eat glass, even though he's twenty-five years out of the service.

↗ **Dear General Patton,**

What kind of gas mileage does this thing get? Is it diesel?

Thanks,

S. Finkter

↗ **Dear S. Finkter,**

No idea on mileage, never seemed important. It is diesel.

Patton

Never seemed important. It will seem important when you run out of gas on the highway where the exits are eighty miles apart and you hear banjo music echoing across the holler.

↗ Gen. Patton,

Okay, I'll just be sure to carry the world's largest gas can with me. I'm sure there's plenty of room for it in the spacious crew compartment.

How about ammo—where do you get it? Does Walmart carry 105mm shells?

S. Finkter

↗ S. Finkter,

The guns are not live and cannot be used.

Patton

No guns? Well, shit. What's the point?

↗ Gen. Patton,

A little bummed about the guns but I understand. As long as the AC and radio work fine, I'm happy.

S. Finkter

↗ S. Finkter,

No AC or radio. This is a tank, not a Chevy.

Patton

Really? We had a Chevy once and it drove like a tank. And not in a good way.

↗ Gen. Patton,

Does that mean there's no iPod hookup?

S. Finkter

95

NAME OUR BABY BOY

LOCATION: Tallahassee, FL

COST: $40,000

DESCRIPTION:

Very simple deal: you pay us $40,000 to set up our baby boy's college fund and we let you give him a first and middle name! We are due in April, so act fast!

It's hard to believe that this lovely young mom-to-be got no bids on this auction! Asking a wealthy stranger to name your baby for forty grand takes some guts, and we're kind of sad that we couldn't make that dream come true for her. We're sure that we could come up with some truly wonderful names for her little cherub. Off the top of our heads:

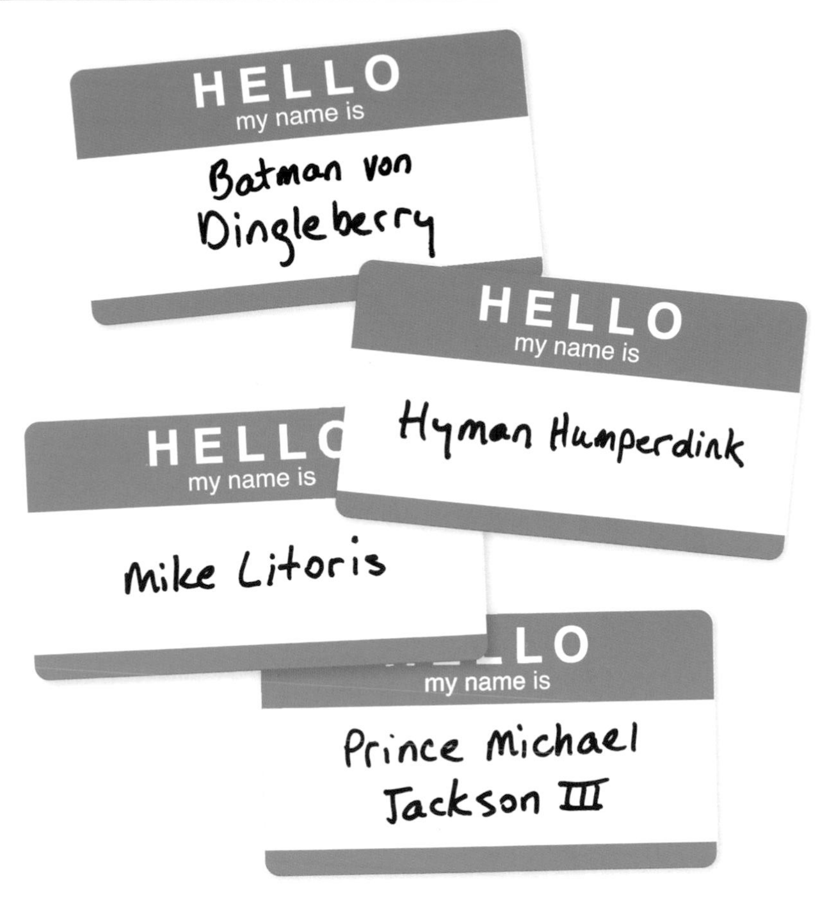

We could go on and on! Naming other people's kids is fun. After all, we won't have to stick around to help the kid get through grammar school saddled with a name that's guaranteed to bring him countless beatings. Even "normal" names earn teasing—that's just par for the elementary school course!

If these parents *had* won $40,000 from some sucker who was dying to name a baby, we only hope they'd consider putting some of that money aside, because therapy is expensive.

96

MECTA 5000Q ELECTRO-CONVULSIVE ECT SHOCK THERAPY SYSTEM

LOCATION:

Arizona, USA

COST:

$1,899

DESCRIPTION:

For sale here is a COMPLETE pre-owned Mecta Spectrum 5000Q ECT Electroconvulsive Therapy System. This device is the newest technology Electro-Convulsive unit available on the market. It is used to treat a variety of psychiatric conditions. This is a complete system!! Includes the Spectrum 5000Q console, Instruction manual, Service Manual, Locking cart, Patient Stimulation Cables, ECG Cable, Sensor input strip, Dynamic load box, and power cord. Also included is a tub of spare parts and disposable supplies to include ECG leads, spare electrodes, gels, etc.

We've been fascinated with electroconvulsive therapy (ECT) ever since we saw Randle McMurphy get strapped and zapped in *One Flew Over the Cuckoo's Nest*. While the treatment did look painful, we're intrigued by the idea that a blast or two of electrical voltage can turn someone foul-tempered or incorrigible into a passive, oblivious drooler. So when we saw this beauty on eBay, we had visions of giving shock treatment to all the prickly people we know—as a favor to them, of course, to improve their quality of life.

We knew no one would volunteer for the treatment, so we decided to offer free massages to our unwitting victims, then wait until they were on the table and fully relaxed before introducing them to the Patient Stimulation Cables. By the time they realized what was happening, it would be too late, and they'd be too stupefied to hurt us. We wrote the seller immediately.

↗ Dear Nurse Ratched,

Hypothetically speaking, is the Mecta 5000Q easy to operate for someone with limited ECT experience? I'm pretty good with mechanical things, and if the manuals are included, I'm confident I can pull it off. I'm anxious to try it on my father-in-law.

S. Finkter

↗ Dear S. Finkter,

I can only sell this machine to a doctor or medical facility. Sorry.

Nurse Ratched

Time to sweeten the deal.

↗ Dear Nurse Ratched,

I certainly understand your hesitation. I'm willing to pay more than your asking price. What if we made it an even $1,900?

S. Finkter

↗ Dear S. Finkter,

I'm sorry, I cannot sell it to you.

Nurse Ratched

Fine, butthole, we'll just get one elsewhere. In the meantime, one more question.

↗ Dear Nurse Ratched,

Would you be interested in a free massage?

S. Finkter

97

AFFORDABLE 3/1 DETROIT MI HOUSE HOME. FREE & CLEAR $7K.

LOCATION:

Detroit, MI

COST:

$7,000 free and clear!

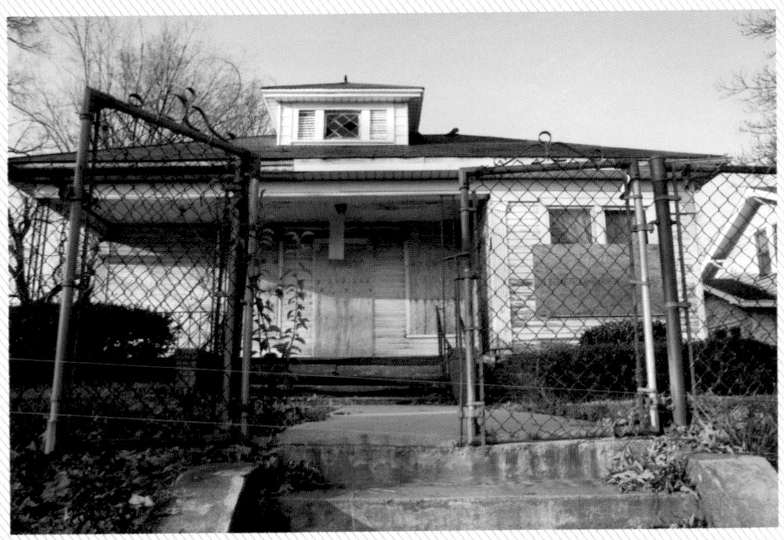

DESCRIPTION:

Single Family Real Estate Rental Income Property 1944. FREE shipping. Now is your chance to own a home. Three bedroom house on .25 acre plot in a busy section of downtown Detroit, close to everything. House needs some TLC. There are no liens—you can own this house outright! Make an offer.

Well, looky here, mama! It's your very own crap shack! For a mere $7,000, you can buy a dilapidated shit hole in what is most likely a crime-ridden ghetto in the fair city of Detroit, MI. We can hardly believe our good fortune!

Seriously, it's a house, and it's not the only one on eBay. There's a whole real estate section full of fancy vacation condos and fire-damaged hovels like this one. We're quite sure that if we were to set foot on this property, we'd have to relocate a few homeless squatters before we'd even cleaned up the crime scene tape and scrubbed the chalk outlines off the floor. After that I'm sure we'd feel right at home, though.

Who buys a house site unseen? Who looks at this picture and says, "Well, it looks a little rough, but boy howdy! That there's a handyman's special!"

Even the picture makes it look as though the inside smells like ten kinds of urine. Without even seeing the flooring, we can tell that there will be stains of questionable (but undeniably organic) origin, and most likely there is mold, suspicious spores, and maybe even a dash of delightful asbestos in the hizzouse. Don't even get us started on the likelihood (no, *probability*) of a very active insect and rodent infestation. Yuck.

Here's a double dare: close your eyes and picture the bathroom. Go ahead, do it. What's the matter? Don't want to envision the cold, stained shitter and crusty bathtub? *Chicken*. We guess it may beat living in a car, but we're not 100 percent sure about that. We've seen some pretty nice cars on eBay going for less than seven grand, and they probably don't even come with bedbugs.

98

HAMSTER COFFIN SWAROVSKI CRYSTAL & STERLING SILVER POTTERY

LOCATION:	COST:
Egg Harbor Township, NJ	$17,950

DESCRIPTION:

One of a kind/handmade! Made from clay slabs, Sterling silver, and Swarovski crystal. For that special departed hamster or mouse that has given you joy. 4 pc. set includes: burial base with 2 large 60ss Swarovski Crystals at either end; Inner cover with 6 Swarovski Crystal Rhinestones; Outer Cover with sterling silver hamster head and sterling silver laminated handle; Bowl of ceramic sunflower seeds to feed your pet on his journey to the afterworld.

This one was a bit out of our price range, and that broke our hearts, because we've always wanted to drop $18K on a ceramic, jewel-encrusted casket for a dead rodent. Doesn't a pet that spent most of its pointless life eating, peeing, and pooping—all in the same place—deserve such a send-off? Absolutely.

So your rodent dies and you put it in this thing—then what? At that price, you're not going to bury it in the backyard. You could put it on display on your mantle, but the smell of rotting vermin carcass can be disconcerting—just ask anyone who has experienced the singular joy of having a rat slough off its rodent coil deep within a wall of his home. The stench does eventually subside within, say, three to four weeks. Your clothing and upholstered furniture will take a bit longer to shake the rot, however, so you may want to pick up some Febreze.

There's a good chance this $18K rat coffin is still for sale on eBay. Before you go snapping it up, though, remember one important fact: rodents go to Hell. It's true. Dead dogs and rabbits go to Heaven, but all other pets—rodents, birds, fish, snakes, turtles, and cats—go directly to the hot place. That means your overpriced fancy rodent coffin will only end up as a canoe in the Lake of Fire. If you don't care, fine, but be good enough to replace the seeds in the casket with some ice cubes. Your little fella will need them in Hell.

99

VBM BILL AIRWAY TRAINER

LOCATION:

Rowlett, TX

COST:

$1,000

DESCRIPTION:

Adult VBM Bill Advanced Airway Simulator/Intubation Trainer. These advanced airway trainers are in good condition. These sell for $2660 at VBM. The VBM Bill Manikin was designed for training in advanced airway management and offers one-stop-shopping for training in virtually every technique including orotracheal intubaton, nasotracheal intubation, all types of cricothyrotomy, fiberoptic intubation, rescue ventilation and more.

Everyone: say hi to Bill. But quietly, please—we don't want to wake him. As you can see, he's had a rough day. He had to take an ice-cold shower this morning because the pilot light went out on his hot water heater. Then he dripped coffee on his favorite tie. Then he slid his convertible under a Mack truck and forgot to duck.

Needless to say, he's not quite feeling like himself today. He can't put his finger on it, but something is missing—including his fingers, which is probably why he can't put one on the problem. We reached out to our seller to get more info on poor Bill.

↗ Dear Jeff Dahmer,

Nice work on the head. How did you get such a nice clean cut? I've tried everything—hacksaw, machete, home-made guillotine—and can't get anything near that clean. What's your secret?

Thanks,

Ed Gein

He didn't reply. Probably doesn't want to divulge his secrets. Serial killers are funny like that. We tried again with a different approach.

↗ Dear Jeff Dahmer,

DUDE! LOVE THAT DOPE FUCKEN HEAD BRO. GOTTA HAVE IT FOR RILZ. WHEN YOU POKE HIS NECK, DOES HE SAY FUNNY CHIT LIKE OW OR GET YOUR PAWS OFF A ME YA DIRTY APES? CUZ HE SHOULD CUZ THAT WOULD BE FUNNY. AND WUTUP WITH $1000 DUDE? DAT BETTER BE A TYPOE BITCH.

Mr. Boneder

Weeks passed with nary a peep. Strike two. We rattled his cage one last time.

↗ Dear Jeff Dahmer,

I am interested in head and this one is very lifelike and handsome. Does his mouth open wider than shown in these photos? Will it curl into an "O" position? Also, how deep is the mouth cavity? Do his eyes open? Eye contact is important.

Thanks,

Leo

Still no answer. We're starting to wonder if the head belonged to the seller himself, although it would be pretty hard to sell your own head on eBay, because how can you pack and ship the thing without eyes?

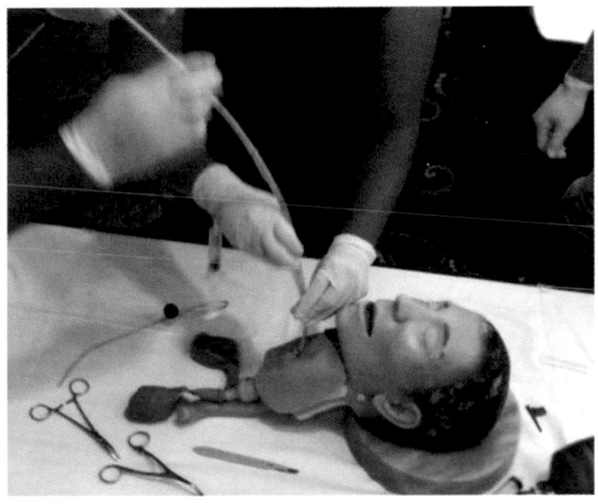

"Brent Spiner (Star Trek: The Next Generation) *gives the performance of his career.* The Head That Wouldn't Say Die (Because His Vocal Cords Were Severed) *is the feel-good movie of the summer. Brilliant!" —Pam Collins, WKOR-TV*

100

GENUINE ROCK—VERY RARE. NFL FOOTBALL.

LOCATION: Gainesville, GA

COST: $2,500

DESCRIPTION:

A natural rock that looks like a hand or Oklahoma. As far as I know, it's the only one in the world. NFL football players or fans, this is the only one. You will never need a voodoo doll again.

Instructions:

1. Take this rock with you to the game.
2. Place on your sideline with the finger pointing to your goal line.
3. Win the game.

Okay, we're fine with selling a rock on eBay. There are lots and lots of rocks being sold on eBay; heck, we even bought a few. But $2,500 for a rock? That, dear friends, is crazy talk.

We're not sure why the seller decided to tie this rock into the NFL, though it does sort of look like one of those big foam fingers you get at the games. Then again, so do actual foam fingers, and we're pretty sure you can get one of those for less than twenty-five hundred clams. For that price, this rock had better come hand-delivered by a celebrity, and maybe with a blowjob thrown in for good measure.

We can think of way better uses for $2,500. If anyone reading this book feels like dropping that kind of money, why not send it our way? We'll have a laugh, cook you something tasty, and maybe take you out to a movie or something. We'll even throw in a foot rub. *That's* a good deal, folks. A rock shaped like Oklahoma: not so much.

101

THE STOCKADE REAR PENETRATION FUCKING MACHINE WITH DILDO

LOCATION:

USA

COST:

$1,000 plus S/H

DESCRIPTION:

This fucking machine restrains the user in a fixed position allowing for optimal rear penetration. The optional waist restraint keeps the hips at the desired height to prevent unwanted movement. The unit controller allows for the user or their master to adjust the speed of the penetration. The fucking rod pivots allowing for many different angles. Quiet, smooth, and easy to use.

Got an extra $1,000 we can borrow? No, not so we can buy this contraption; we're gonna need money for the electric shock therapy we'll need in order to get this image out of our heads. Let's talk this out, shall we?

It's probably a bondage thing, hence the name "Stockade" and the fact that her ankles and wrists are bound. So couples of both sexes probably use it together, right? Or maybe it's something you'd find in a dominatrix's . . . what? Lair?

Perhaps one buys this machine because one is single, but still needs a good pounding in the rear entrance every so often. We really hope not, because that would make us wonder if every lonely spinster we've ever known secretly has a torture chamber of bondage devices in her house somewhere. Please don't make us visualize our cat-lady coworker getting rear-ended by a piece of Nautilus equipment. Please?

Speaking of gym equipment, this fucking machine looks like the type of thing that looks great online, but once you get it home and the excitement of having it wears off, you're left with a bulky hunk of metal in your living room. It takes up a lot of space and seldom gets used, and its very presence reminds you that you're a slacker who should be mechanically pounding yourself in the ass much more often. Before long, you're hanging stuff on it and then it becomes nothing more than a thousand-dollar coat rack.

But it's not a coat rack, it's a fucking machine. A machine that fucks you. We may consider buying it if it also performs some other useful functions, like mashing potatoes or rocking the baby's cradle or making ice cream. What a fun summer treat! Just replace the dildo with a metal beater and whip up some homemade Rocky Road. Then, while the kids are busy eating their dessert, the dildo goes back on and mommy slips away to a little place called Pleasure Town.

Come to think of it, maybe we *do* have an extra thousand bucks lying around.

ABOUT THE AUTHORS

Cary McNeal is an Emmy®-winning television producer and writer. He is the author of *1,001 Facts that Will Scare the S*!t Out of You* and has written comedy for Mike Myers, Jackie Chan, and Fred Williard. Visit him at www.listoftheday.net.

Beverly Jenkins is an award-winning TV producer, director, and writer. She lives in New Hampshire. Visit her at www.blinzerjenkins.com.

ACKNOWLEDGMENTS

This book would not exist without the brilliance and kindness of many people, including: Holly Schmidt and Allan Penn at Hollan Publishing; Jordana Tusman at Running Press; Perry and Jean McNeal; Cyndi Culpepper; Connie Biltz; Burt Wolff, Wayne Overstreet, and everyone at Wolff Bros. Post in Atlanta; and all my friends at List of the Day. A special thanks goes to my friend and co-author, Beverly Linzer Jenkins, for her hard work and inspiration. Most of all, I thank my girls, Paige and Keaton, for their unconditional love and support.

—Cary

I'd like to thank the following people for their support: my guys—Jim, Daniel, and Matthew. Deborah Smith, Mala Tyler, and Laurie Laizure, for all of their advice and encouragement. Doug and Wanda Linzer and Jenkins South for their undying love and guidance. A huge thank-you to the fabulous Holly Schmidt and Allan Penn at Hollan Publishing; Jordana Tusman at Running Press; my Hestia friends; and all of my blog BOOBHs, who are spectacular. Last but not least, many thanks to my friend and co-author, Cary McNeal, for everything.

—Beverly